D1736816

PRINT'S BEST ILLUSTRATION & PHOTOGRAPHY

PRINT'S BEST ILLUSTRATION & PHOTOGRAPHY

Library of Congress Catalog Card Number 93-084080
ISBN 0-915734-82-6

RC PUBLICATIONS

President and Publisher: Howard Cadel
Vice President and Editor: Martin Fox
Creative Director: Andrew Kner
Managing Director, Book Projects: Linda Silver
Associate Art Director: Nell Coyle
Administrative Assistant: Nancy Silver

Print's Best

ILLUSTRATION & PHOTOGRAPHY

WINNING DESIGNS FROM PRINT MAGAZINE'S NATIONAL COMPETITION

Edited by

LINDA SILVER

Designed by

ANDREW KNER

Introduction by

JULIE LASKY

Published by

RC PUBLICATIONS, INC.
NEW YORK, NY

INTRODUCTION

Photography and illustration serve several functions in graphic design, few of them exclusive. The art may be the dominant focus of the communication or a supplemental feature. It may draw the eye to a designated spot on the page like a magnet, condense the theme of an article like a headline, or unglue the viewer like a solvent. Its purpose may be to incite observers to act (shop, donate money to a charity, attend the theater) or lure them into repose (a comfortable chair and a good read).

This is to say, however many clichéd words a picture may be worth, an image that stands alone can never tell the whole story in graphic design. Even if art directors commission the most spectacular photograph ever shot or the most compelling illustration ever rendered, they must still solve the problem of integrating type into their layouts, not to mention ensuring that the final configuration and production of the piece does justice to both the artist's craft and to the concept it was intended to serve. For that reason, the photography and illustration that appear in this latest addition to PRINT's Best series enhance—and are in turn enhanced by—all the supporting elements in their designs. Culled from recent issues of PRINT's Regional Design Annual, the more than 200 photographs and illustrations shown here pay tribute to the skills of scores of artists. More important, each is a vital part of a communication that is visually and conceptually unified; and thus each is displayed in the venue for which it was created—page, package, book jacket, shopping bag, billboard, or poster.

More than a distillation of work that has appeared in the Regional, this book is a celebration of the range of photography and illustration currently produced. The design of a public service advertisement as compared to, say, a compact disk package demands a different artistic solution—so different that one can rest assured that nothing that challenges the diversity of visual expression these days, neither the tendency of artists to plunder the past (and each other) for ideas, nor the clichés encouraged by computer-generated imagery, will rob photography and illustration of its variety. As long as graphic designers are offered a vast number of problems to solve, and as long as they, along with

CONTENTS

the designers who hire them, seek appropriate solutions, a documentary photo of a homeless couple and a computer-manipulated portrait of a rock band will cohabitate happily in collections such as this one.

Even more encouraging, this book reveals the efforts of artists to reinvent old forms and to experiment with technology. A photographic sequence of cows that differ only in the vibrant coloring of their spots brings Andy Warhol to mind, but it's also an awfully good way of visualizing the many different flavors in a line of schnapps. And if a wrapped delivery truck advertising an overnight postal service owes even the vaguest debt to Christo, who cares? The image looks fresh and conveys its message with the staccato impact required of advertising art.

The Mac may be blamed for too many popsicle-colored, rasterized images in our society, but we can thank it for helping to collapse the once distinct genres of photography and illustration into a form that transcends category. The growing tendency of artists to manipulate and collage images in the computer, doodle on their photographs, or incorporate snapshots into their paintings isn't new to the world of studio art, but it's finding increasing acceptance in all areas of graphic design—even annual reports—where clients once depended on illustration to tell a story and on photography to tell the truth. Photo-illustration extends the artist's range of visual expression, but its complexity is more than esthetic; viewers are being asked, once and for all, to drop any assumption that photography is an objective science and that drawing and painting are subjective arts. The hand—the artist's unique signature—is being given as much credence as the eye and lens when it comes to interpreting a client's product or activity.

Whether they express themselves through a tightly rendered watercolor, a reckless swipe of a bamboo pen, or a raw-edged Polaroid, many of the artists in this book reveal individual styles. Part of the pleasure in reviewing the contents is seeing how they adapt them to different assignments, for graphic design is, ultimately, a confluence of identities and visions. Many minds contribute to the moment when the unsuspecting viewer turns a page or surveys a shelf and is walloped by color, wit, poignancy, terror, lusciousness, or nostalgia.—*Julie Lasky*

The ◆ accompanying many of the visuals indicates which are the 1992 Regional Annual winners.

American Society of Magazine Photographers (Dallas Chapter)

Promotional poster.

DESIGN FIRM:

Eisenberg and Associates,

Dallas, Texas

CREATIVE DIRECTOR:

Arthur Eisenberg

ART DIRECTOR/

DESIGNER: Saul Torres

PHOTOGRAPHER:

Scott Metcalfe

1992 cover illustration for lobbying group directory and cover of 1990 edition. ART DIRECTOR/ DESIGNER/ILLUSTRATOR: Gayle Kabaker, Rowayton, Connecticut

The 1990 National Organic Wholesalers Directory and Yearbook
ORGANIC FOOD & FARM SUPPLIES

Editorial spreads.

DESIGN FIRM:

Arizona Highways,

Phoenix, Arizona

CREATIVE DIRECTOR:

Gary Bennett

ART DIRECTOR/

DESIGNER: Christine Mitchell

PHOTOGRAPHER: Tom Till

PICTURE EDITOR:

Peter Ensenberger

EDITOR: Robert J. Early

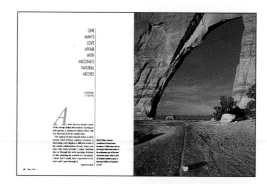

A PORTFOLIO
Continued from page 28

*O*ne of the state's most unusual places to find natural arches is in the deep, sinuous complex of slot canyons in northern Arizona. In some areas, flash-flood waters channeled through the narrow passage have sculpted small arches in sandstone fins high above the canyon floors. Despite their size, these arches appear to meet all the requirements of those who catalog and count these anomalies, and their delicate beauty is the match of any of their larger cousins.

I have heard stories about a giant lost arch somewhere on the Vermilion Cliffs. I doubt it has escaped discovery by cowboys, hikers, or pilots all these years, but it could be there, hidden in some majestic alcove, or some forgotten canyon.

Even if no more great arches are found, Arizona always will be a treasure trove for arch lovers. From Lake Mead to the Petrified Forest National Park and from Organ Pipe Cactus National Monument to Monument Valley, nearly 100 rock openings dot the Arizona landscape. With that many to experience and photograph, my work will never be done.

Photo Tour: Join the Friends of *Arizona Highways* and author-photographer Tom Till on a photo exploration of magnificent Monument Valley, October 1-3. This popular trip fills quickly, so it's not too soon to make plans. For information and reservations, call the Friends' Travel Desk, (602) 271-5904.

Photographer Tom Till lives in Moab, Utah, just outside Arches National Park, the perfect location from which to pursue his passion for natural arches. He is working on a scenic book New Jersey, Images of Nature, for Westcliffe Publishers.

(PRECEDING PANEL, PAGES 30 AND 31) As if perched on the nose of a giant being, the Spectacles Arch peers across Monument Valley.
(RIGHT) This fancifully shaped formation in Monument Valley is aptly called Ear of the Wind Arch.

THE QUARTERLY COMMUNICATION OF
THE DECORATIVE CENTER HOUSTON

2

Summer 1991

Front page of newsletter.

AGENCY: Geer Design/

Boswell Byers Advertising,

Houston, Texas

ART DIRECTOR: Mark Geer

DESIGNER/ILLUSTRATOR:

Morgan Bomar

DCH

Decorative Center of Houston (Residential/Commercial Furnishing Showrooms)

TO IMAGINE WHAT THE NEW OMNIMAX THEATER IS LIKE,
TAKE THIS AD AND WRAP IT AROUND YOUR HEAD.

It's got a four-story-high domed screen. State-of-the-art audio. And a unique 70MM projection system. So at the new Omnimax theater, you don't just watch movies. You're part of them. And the Anheuser-Busch Foundation is proud to help sponsor this amazing new part of the St. Louis Science Center. We hope you'll join us for the grand opening November 2nd.

ANHEUSER-BUSCH
FOUNDATION

Anheuser-Busch Foundation

Promotional ad.

AGENCY: DMB&B/St. Louis,

St. Louis, Missouri

GROUP CREATIVE

DIRECTOR: Tom Gow

CREATIVE DIRECTOR:

Greg Sullentrup

ART DIRECTOR: Jenni Holt

PHOTOGRAPHER: Stock

COPYWRITER: Harry Hayes

PRODUCTION MANAGER:

Karl Lemp

In 1979, almost 350 years after the Rev. William Blaxton planted America's first apple orchard in Boston, some hopeful growers planted Arizona's first commercial apple orchard near Wilcox. About the same time, smaller family-owned orchards took root in the Sulphur Springs Valley near Willcox and in other parts of the state.

Apples Apples Apples

There's fruit to pick, fresh cider to drink at Arizona's orchards

Text by Jan Barstad and Jack Stephens
Photographs by Randy Prentice
Maps and Illustration by John B. Murdock

Opening spread.

DESIGN FIRM:

Arizona Highways,

Phoenix, Arizona

CREATIVE DIRECTOR:

Gary Bennett

ART DIRECTOR:

Christine Mitchell

ASSOCIATE ART

DIRECTOR/DESIGNER:

Mary Velgos

PHOTOGRAPHER:

Randy Prentice

ILLUSTRATOR:

John B. Murdock

PICTURE EDITOR:

Peter Ensenberger

EDITOR: Robert J. Early

New Year's season

shopping bag.

ILLUSTRATOR:

Philippe Lardy, New York,

New York

DESIGN FIRM:

Bloomingdale's

CREATIVE DIRECTOR:

John C. Jay

ART DIRECTOR: Jim Christie

Promotional ad announcing

new location.

AGENCY: The Knape Group,

Dallas, Texas

ART DIRECTORS:

Michael Connors, Willie

Baronet

DESIGNER/ILLUSTRATOR/

COPYWRITER:

Michael Connors

COPYWRITER: Shari Landa

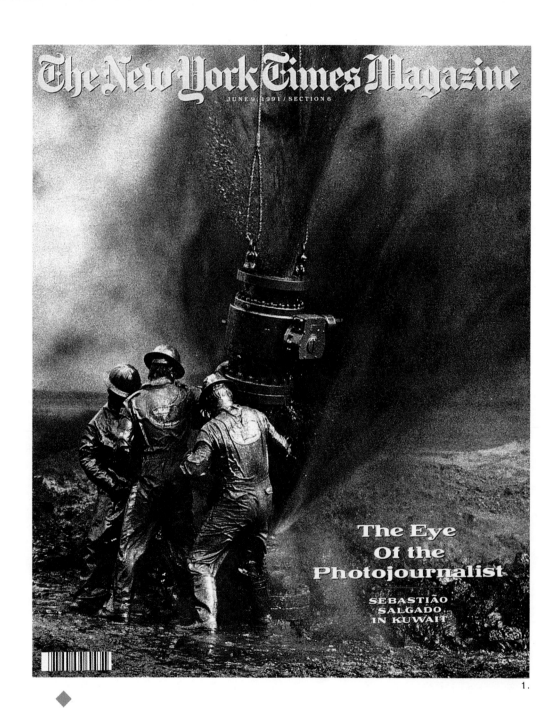

1.

Sunday supplement covers.

DESIGN FIRM:

The New York Times

Magazine, New York,

New York

ART DIRECTOR:

Janet Froelich

DESIGNERS: Janet Froelich

(1), Kandy Littrell (2)

PHOTOGRAPHER:

Sebastiao Salgado (1)

PHOTO EDITOR:

Kathy Ryan (1)

ILLUSTRATOR:

Charles Burns (2)

2.

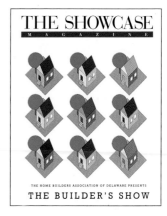

Kick-off publication for

Builder's Show.

DESIGN FIRM:

Miller Mauro Group,

Wilmington, Delaware

ART DIRECTOR:

Jon McPheeters

DESIGNERS: Andy Cruz,

Jon McPheeters

ILLUSTRATOR: Andy Cruz

THE ARTS

IBM

Illustration and spreads

from corporate brochure.

DESIGN FIRM:

Pentagram Design, New

York, New York

ART DIRECTOR/

DESIGNER: Susan Hochbaum

ILLUSTRATOR:

James McMullan

Anheuser-Busch, Inc.

Ads for Budweiser.

AGENCY: DMB&B/St. Louis,

St. Louis, Missouri

GROUP CREATIVE

DIRECTOR: Mark Choate

CREATIVE DIRECTORS:

Ric Anello (1,2), Tom

Hudder (3)

ART DIRECTORS:

Scott O'Leary (1,2), Tom

Hudder (3)

PHOTOGRAPHERS:

Brian Lanker (1,2), Greg

Stroube (3)

COPYWRITERS:

John Krueger (1,2), Peter

McCarty (3)

PRODUCTION MANAGER:

Ed Layton

HIT THE HEAVY BAG.

———

SPEED BAG.

———

SHOWERS.

———

FRIDGE.

NOTHING BEATS A BUDWEISER

1.

ALWAYS TREAT

———

SCRAPES AND BRUISES

———

WITH SOMETHING

———

VERY COLD.

NOTHING BEATS A BUDWEISER

2.

Front.   Back.   Upside Down.   Backwards.

Right Side.   Top.

Left Side.   Bottom.

No Matter How You Look At It, Nothing Beats A Bud.
Friends Know When To Say When

3.

Ad campaign.

AGENCY: Ammirati & Puris, New York, New York

ART DIRECTORS: Nan Hutchison, James Dalthorp (2)

PHOTOGRAPHER: Lamb & Hall

COPYWRITER: Larry Goldstein

Just this once, we'd like to give our vehicles the image they deserve.

Of course you won't see any of our drivers making deliveries in anything like this. You will however notice the speed at which our ground service works.

Quite simply, UPS offers the fastest scheduled ground delivery serving the forty-eight states today. In fact, of the ten million packages we deliver each day, four million are overnight ground deliveries. And when you couple that with our well proven record for on-time reliability, you can rest assured that your packages will consistently arrive at the time they are scheduled to arrive. All within the legal speed limits.

So why ship with anyone else but UPS. After all, with 64,000 vehicles on the road and eighty-four years of experience, it's no wonder our service is what some might call, well, up to speed. **We run the tightest ship in the shipping business.**

1.

Every day, ten million ground packages arrive in this shape.

Each day, UPS is entrusted with delivering more packages than any other ground delivery service. But when you take into consideration our well proven record for on-time reliability, it's no small wonder that over a million businesses rely upon our familiar brown package cars.

In fact, with as many as 64,000 vehicles on the road daily, we offer the fastest, most efficient ground delivery service to every single address in the lower forty-eight states. Knowing all that, it's quite easy to understand why UPS continues to be the most widely used ground carrier.

So when you send your package with UPS, you'll not only know when it will arrive but also exactly what shape it'll arrive in. **We run the tightest ship in the shipping business.**

2.

ONE AGAINST THE WIND

Judy Davis and Sam Neill in "One Against the Wind"
The 170th Presentation of the Hallmark Hall of Fame
Premieres Sunday, December 1, 1991 on CBS-Television

Closed Captioned for the Hearing Impaired.

Hallmark
Hall of Fame

40th Anniversary
1951-1991

Promotional poster for television movie.

DESIGN FIRM:
Muller & Company, Kansas City, Missouri
ART DIRECTOR/
DESIGNER: John Muller
ASSISTANT ART
DIRECTOR: Scott Chapman
ILLUSTRATOR:
Mark English

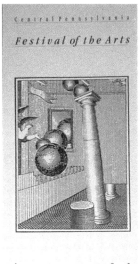

Poster (1) and call-for-entries brochures (2,3) for annual summer arts festival.

DESIGN FIRM:

Sommese Design, State College, Pennsylvania

ART DIRECTOR/

DESIGNER/ILLUSTRATOR:

Lanny Sommese

DESIGNER: Mark Smith (2,3)

1.

2.

3.

Poster publicizing talk by designer Woody Pirtle.

DESIGN FIRM: Pentagram Design, New York, New York

ART DIRECTOR/ DESIGNER: Woody Pirtle

DESIGNER: Matt Heck

PHOTOGRAPHER: Bill Whitehurst

HEAVEN CAN'T WAIT
By Ed Lindlof   *For information about programs on the afterlife, see View More About It on page 52.*

1.

Pages and detail from TDC magazine.

DESIGN FIRM:

TDC Magazine, Bethesda, Maryland

ART DIRECTOR:

John Lyle Sanford

ILLUSTRATORS:

Ed Lindlof (1), Guy Billout (3), Sheldon Greenberg (2, 4)

2.

SHOCK WAVE OF THE FUTURE
By Guy Billout   *For information about programs on tsunamis, see View More About It on page 54.*

3.

CUSTER'S LAST MISUNDERSTANDING: JUNE 25th, 1876
By Sheldon Greenberg

4.

Direct mail campaign.

DESIGN FIRM: Star Tribune,

Minneapolis, Minnesota

ART DIRECTOR/

DESIGNER:

Kimberly Dziubinski

ILLUSTRATOR: Stan Olsen

COPYWRITER:

Gary Nylander

SOMEHOW, REX KNEW HE DIDN'T FIT IN.

IT OCCURS TO THE GREAT ZAMBENI THAT
TIMING IS EVERYTHING.

ANGELA WAKES UP TO THE FACTS, SLOWLY.

IT DIDN'T TAKE JOE LONG TO DECIDE TO
TRY SOMETHING DIFFERENT.

Benjamin Publishing Co., Inc. (Fine Art/Photography Publishing)

Book jacket (1) and spreads (2,3) from *Isles of Eden.*

DESIGN FIRM: Modino, New York, New York

ART DIRECTOR: Maureen O'Brien

DESIGNER: Dean Papparlardo

PHOTOGRAPHER: Harvey Lloyd (1)

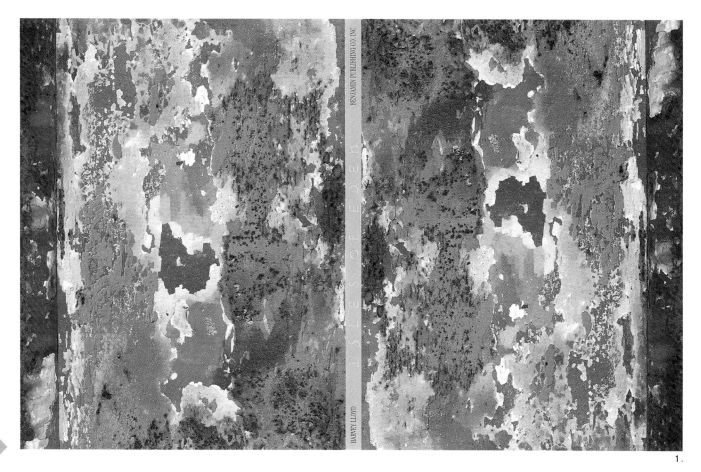

1.

2.

3.

Sunday supplement cover.

DESIGN FIRM:

The Boston Globe

Magazine, Boston,

Massachusetts

ART DIRECTOR/

DESIGNER:

 Lucy Bartholomay

ILLUSTRATOR:

Malcolm Tarlofsky

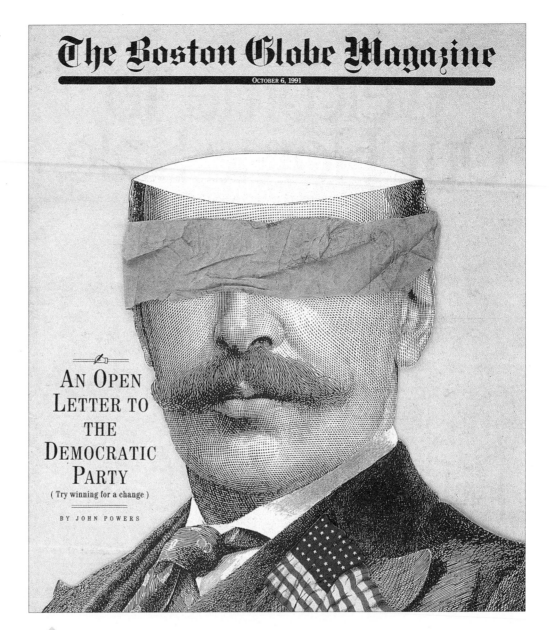

Self-promotional postcards.

DESIGN FIRM: Wet Inc.,

Phoenix, Maryland

DESIGNER/ILLUSTRATOR:

Mike McConnell

Cover (1) and spreads (3,4)

from 1991 annual report.

DESIGN FIRM:

New View Studios,

Rosemont, Illinois

ART DIRECTORS:

Greg Samata, Pat Samata

PHOTOGRAPHER:

Sandro D. Miller

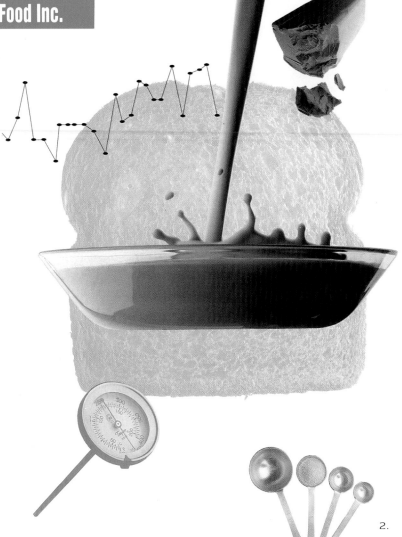

2.

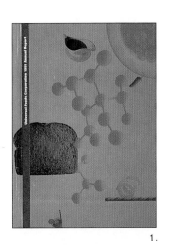

1.

3.

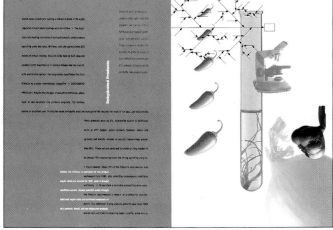

4.

Karl Denham (Illustration)

Self-promotional ad (1), and postcards (2,3) and envelopes (4,5) for direct-mail self-promotion campaign.

DESIGN FIRM:
Karl Denham, Hoboken, New Jersey

DESIGNER:
Melissa Wasserman

ILLUSTRATOR:
Karl Denham

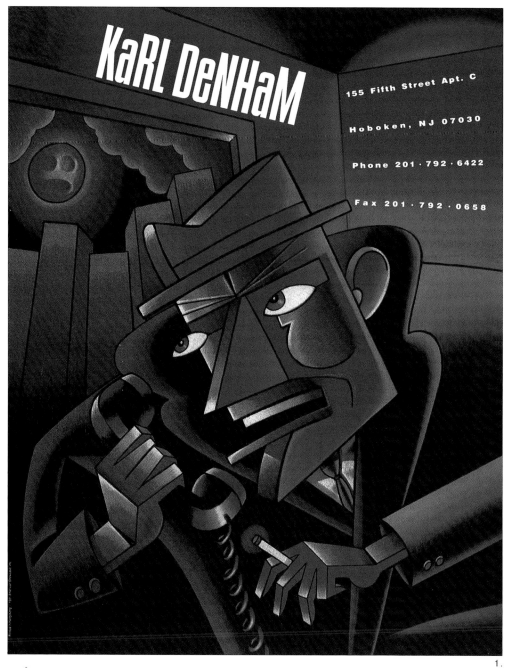

KaRL DeNHaM

155 Fifth Street Apt. C

Hoboken, NJ 07030

Phone 201·792·6422

Fax 201·792·0658

1.

2.

3.

4.

5.

CD cover and disk.

DESIGN FIRM:

Warner Bros. Records,

Burbank, California

ART DIRECTORS:

Anthony Kiedis, Kim

Champagne

DESIGNER: Kim Champagne

PHOTOGRAPHER:

Gus Van Zant

ILLUSTRATOR:

Henk Schiftmaker

Warner Bros. Records

**Gene Federico
Profile of an American Master**

After graduating from Pratt
Institute in 1938, Gene Federico
worked for a small advertising
agency in New York. This bud-
ding career was interrupted by
service with the U.S. Army,
where he continued to design
murals and posters and orga-
nized an exhibition of soldiers'
paintings in Oran. After the war
he worked successively for
Grey Advertising, Doyle Dane
Bernbach, Benton and Bowles,
and Warwick and Legler, until
1967 when he helped found
Lord, Geller, Federico, Einstein
Inc. Federico creates advertising campaigns and corporate
images in all media. His many
awards include those of the New
York Art Directors Club, the
American Institute of Graphic
Arts and the Type Directors
Club of New York. His work was
shown in an exhibition of international graphic design in
London in 1978. In November
1980 he was inducted into
the Art Directors Club Hall of
Fame and was the recipient of
the AIGA gold medal in 1987.

This is the first in a series of
lectures on American Masters
in graphic design presented by
the New York Chapter of the
American Institute of Graphic
Arts, AIGA/NY.

**Wednesday 7:00 pm
25 March 1992**
Fashion Institute of Technology
Katie Murphy Amphitheatre
227 West 27th Street at
Seventh Avenue, New York City

Admission
$5 AIGA/NY members
$10 general public
AIGA/NY student members
and FIT students free
$3 other students with valid ID

Poster publicizing talk by
designer Gene Federico.
DESIGN FIRM:
Pentagram Design, New
York, New York
ASSOCIATE/DESIGNER :
Michael Gericke
PHOTOGRAPHER:
Jerry Friedman
TYPOGRAPHER: Typogram
PRINTER: Terwilliger/
Sterling-Roman

American Institute of Graphic Arts

31

Promotional poster for
Mystery! television series.
DESIGN FIRM:
Paul Davis Studio, New
York, New York
DESIGNER/ILLUSTRATOR:
Paul Davis
ART DIRECTOR:
Fran Michelman/Mobil

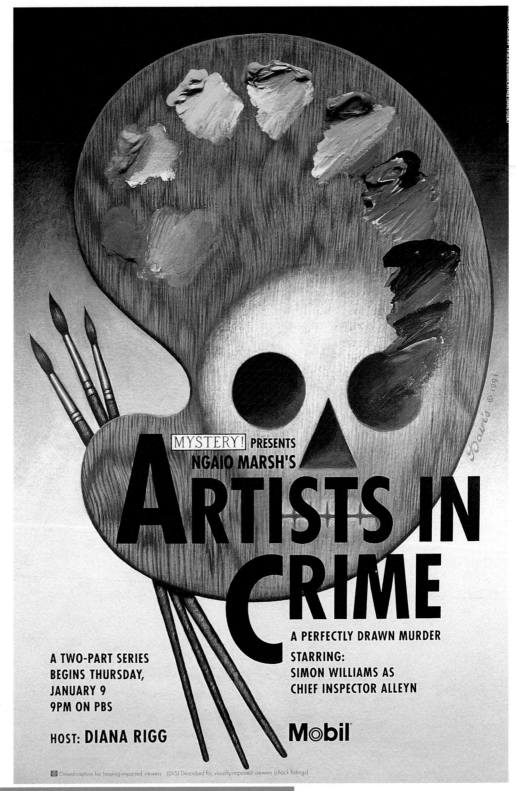

MYSTERY! PRESENTS
NGAIO MARSH'S
ARTISTS IN CRIME
A PERFECTLY DRAWN MURDER
STARRING:
SIMON WILLIAMS AS
CHIEF INSPECTOR ALLEYN

A TWO-PART SERIES
BEGINS THURSDAY,
JANUARY 9
9PM ON PBS

HOST: DIANA RIGG

Mobil

Closed-caption for hearing-impaired viewers (DVS) Described for visually-impaired viewers (check listings)

Mobil Oil Corporation

Poster protesting American
military involvement in
Kuwait and Iraq.
DESIGN FIRM:
Saint Hieronymus Press,
Inc., Berkeley, California
ART DIRECTOR/
DESIGNER/ILLUSTRATOR:
David Lance Goines

Pro Bono Publico

GOOD ARCHITECTURE IS

LIKE A PIECE OF BEAUTIFULLY

COMPOSED MUSIC, CRYSTAL-

LIZED IN SPACE THAT

ELEVATES OUR SPIRITS

BEYOND THE LIMITATION

OF TIME.

Tao Ho

FALLING WATER IS ENERGY, a community which brings the best of two worlds together—the quiet tranquility of the Village of Burr Ridge and the vibrant cosmopolitan city of Chicago. That energy is a foundation for a well-rounded life. Falling Water provides opportunities for people who lead an active, outdoor-oriented life with easy access to prominent golf courses, world-class polo facilities, tennis and swimming clubs. The broad canvas of intellectual, artistic and cultural activities are served by a fine collection of public and private schools, theatre, the symphony and ballet. Falling Water attracts people like you—people who seek both gracious living and the good life . . . people who know the difference between making a living and building a life.

Falling Water . . . in Burr Ridge. It's the best of both worlds.

IT SEEMS TO ME THAT THERE WOULD

BE A CERTAIN PLEASURE IN THINKING

THAT YOU HAD UTILIZED YOUR LIFE

WELL, LEARNED AS MUCH AS YOU

COULD, GATHERED IN AS MUCH AS

POSSIBLE OF THE UNIVERSE, AND

ENJOYED IT.

Isaac Asimov

Cover and spreads from sales brochure.

DESIGN FIRM:

Hill and Knowlton, Inc.,

Chicago, Illinois

ART DIRECTOR:

Andrew Brown

DESIGNERS: Mary Ackerly,

Andrew Brown

PHOTOGRAPHER:

Laurie Rubin

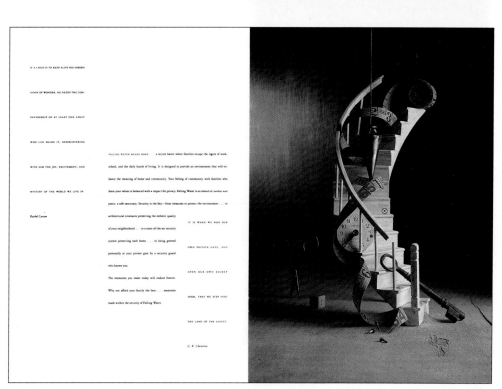

IF A CHILD IS TO KEEP ALIVE HIS INBORN

SENSE OF WONDER, HE NEEDS THE COM-

PANIONSHIP OF AT LEAST ONE ADULT

WHO CAN SHARE IT, REDISCOVERING

WITH HIM THE JOY, EXCITEMENT, AND

MYSTERY OF THE WORLD WE LIVE IN.

Rachel Carson

FALLING WATER MEANS HOME . . . a secure haven where families escape the rigors of work, school, and the daily hustle of living. It is designed to provide an environment that will enhance the meaning of home and community. Your feeling of community with families who share your values is balanced with a respect for privacy. Falling Water is an island of comfort and peace, a safe sanctuary. Security is the key—from measures to protect the environment . . . to architectural covenants preserving the esthetic quality of your neighborhood . . . to a state-of-the-art security system protecting each home . . . to being greeted personally at your private gate by a security guard who knows you.

The memories you make today will endure forever. Why not afford your family the best . . . memories made within the security of Falling Water.

IT IS WHEN WE PASS OUR

OWN PRIVATE GATE, AND

OPEN OUR OWN SECRET

DOOR, THAT WE STEP INTO

THE LAND OF THE GIANTS.

G. K. Chesterton

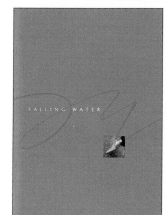

FALLING WATER

Pacific-Sakata Development Inc. (Real Estate Development)

New Zealand somewhere under the rainbow

A PHOTOGRAPHY EXHIBIT BY JACK KENNER ♦ APRIL 1 - AUGUST 31 ♦ AT MEMPHIS INTERNATIONAL AIRPORT ♦ PRINTS SPONSORED BY MEMPHIS ENGRAVING, INC ♦ A MEMPHIS IN MAY SANCTIONED EVENT IN COLLABORATION WITH "ARTS IN THE AIRPORT"

♦ POSTER CONCEPT & DESIGN BY BRIAN GROPPE / TOWERY PUBLISHING, INC. ♦ SEPARATIONS & IMAGE COMPOSITION BY MEMPHIS ENGRAVING, INC. ♦ PRINTING BY PENNACLE PRESS ♦ PRINTED ON GOLDEN CASK 80# COVER FROM ATHENS PAPER, CO. ♦ © JACK KENNER 1993 ♦

Poster promoting arts festival exhibit.

PHOTOGRAPHER: Jack Kenner, Memphis, Tennessee

DESIGN FIRM: Memphis Engraving

DESIGNER: Brian Groppe

SEPARATIONS & IMAGE COMPOSITIONS: Memphis Engraving

PRINTER: Pennacle Press

Originally a point-of-purchase display for Nestlé; then used as a self-promotion piece.

ILLUSTRATOR:

Alex Murawski,

Watkinsville, Georgia

DESIGN FIRM:

Langworth Taylor

ART DIRECTOR/

DESIGNER:

Francesca D'Esterno

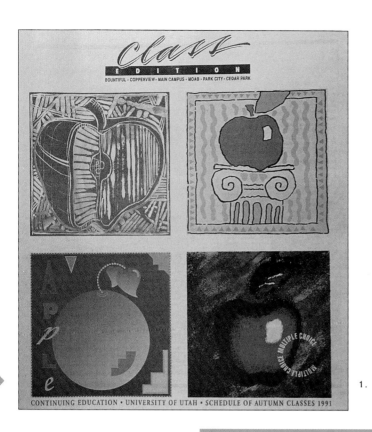

1.

Front (1) and back (2) covers and spread (3) from the division's course catalog.

DESIGN FIRM: DCE Design, University of Utah, Salt Lake City, Utah

ART DIRECTOR: Scott Greer

DESIGNER: Stephen Tuft

ILLUSTRATORS: Tim Peterson, Lisa Brashear, Stephen Tuft, Michael Schoenfeld, Kathy Schmidt

University of Utah Continuing Education Division

2.

3.

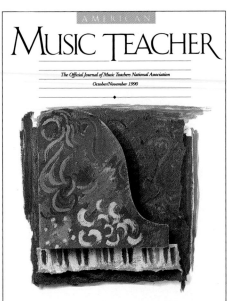

Magazine covers.

DESIGN FIRM:

Libby Perszyk Kathman,

Cincinnati, Ohio

ART DIRECTORS:

Diane De Villez, Bluford Moor

DESIGNER/ILLUSTRATOR:

Liz Kathman Grubow.

PHOTOGRAPHER:

Alan Brown/Photonics

US Brick (Consumer/Commercial Brick Manufacturer)

Truck graphics.

DESIGN FIRM:

Warren/Martino, Austin,

Texas

ART DIRECTORS:

Lauri Worthington,

Kanokwalee Lee

ILLUSTRATORS:

Doug Jaques, Gary Martin,

Linda Jaques

Magazine cover.

DESIGN FIRM: Ms. Magazine,

New York, New York

ART DIRECTOR/

DESIGNER: Nancy Smith

ILLUSTRATOR:

Janet Woolley

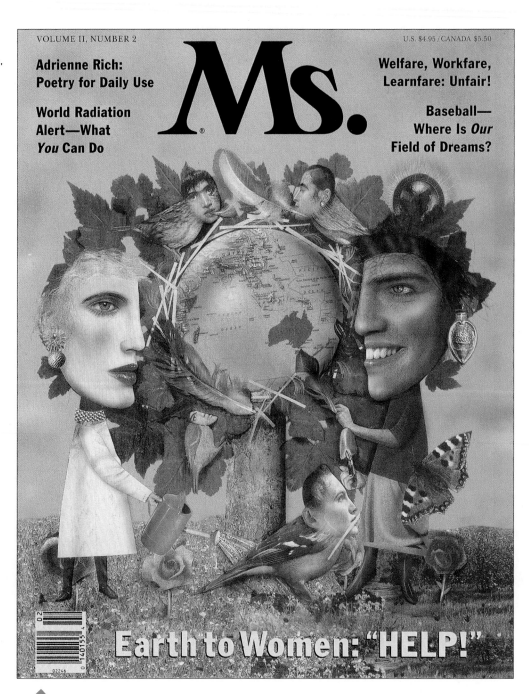

VOLUME II, NUMBER 2

U.S. $4.95 / CANADA $5.50

**Adrienne Rich:
Poetry for Daily Use**

**World Radiation
Alert—What
You Can Do**

Ms.

**Welfare, Workfare,
Learnfare: Unfair!**

**Baseball—
Where Is *Our*
Field of Dreams?**

Earth to Women: "HELP!"

Book cover.

DESIGN FIRM: Pantheon,

New York, New York

ART DIRECTOR/

DESIGNER:

Marjorie Anderson

ILLUSTRATOR:

Lars Hokanson

Ad campaign.

AGENCY: Fallon McElligott,

Minneapolis, Minnesota

ART DIRECTOR: Arty Tan

PHOTOGRAPHER: Marvy!,

Hopkins, Minnesota

COPYWRITER: Bill Miller

DeKuyper (Beverage Manufacturer)

Key Largo Tropical Schnapps. And over 40 other delicious shades, too.

Buttershots Butterscotch Schnapps. And a herd of over 40 other flavors.

Ad campaign.

AGENCY:

Hoffman York & Compton,

Milwaukee, Wisconsin

CREATIVE DIRECTOR:

Tom Jordan

ART DIRECTOR/

DESIGNER:

Michael J. Wheaton

PHOTOGRAPHER:

Dennis Manarchy

COPYWRITERS:

Tom Jordan, Reed Allen (3),

Michael J. Wheaton (1,2)

RETOUCHER:

Paintbox/Altered Images

1.

2.

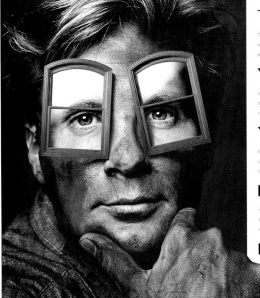

3.

Cécilene (Mail Order)

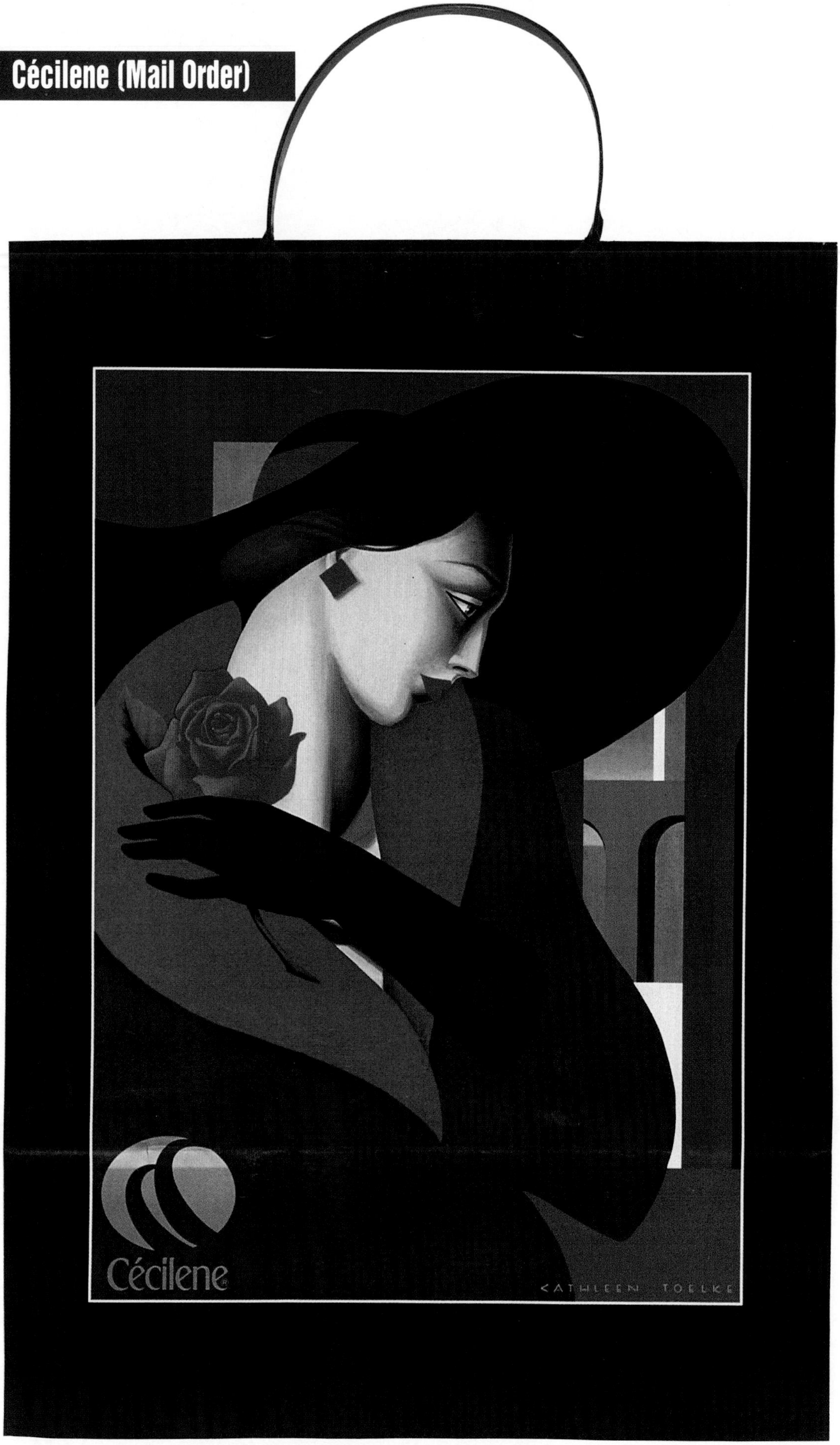

Shopping bag.

ILLUSTRATOR:

Cathleen Toelke,

Rhinebeck, New York

AGENCY: Hakuhodo, Inc.

ART DIRECTOR:

Shuzo Hirata

THE
Bee

Text by Dr. Beth B. Norden
Illustrations by
Biruta
Akerbergs
Hansen

Dimensional
Nature
Portfolio
Series

Cover and spread from pop-
up book.

DESIGN FIRM:

Stewart, Tabori & Chang,

Inc., New York, New York

ART DIRECTOR:

Jim Wageman

COVER DESIGNER:

Lynn Pieroni

ILLUSTRATOR:

Biruta Akersbergs Hansen

BOOK DESIGNERS:

Lynette Ruschak,

James Diaz

Stewart, Tabori & Chang (Publishing)

Covers of advertising supplements—one for the 1991 boat show (1) and one for the Minnesota Guide Home Update(2).

DESIGN FIRM:
Minneapolis Star Tribune, Minneapolis, Minnesota

ART DIRECTOR/
DESIGNER: Lynn Phelps

ILLUSTRATORS:
Roy Pendelton (1), Steven Guarnaccia (2)

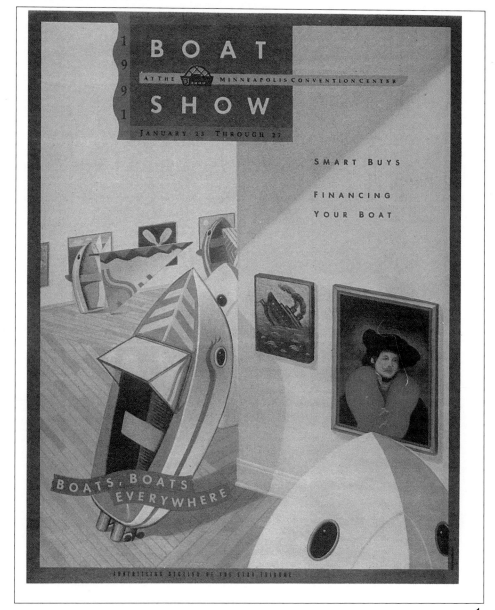

1.

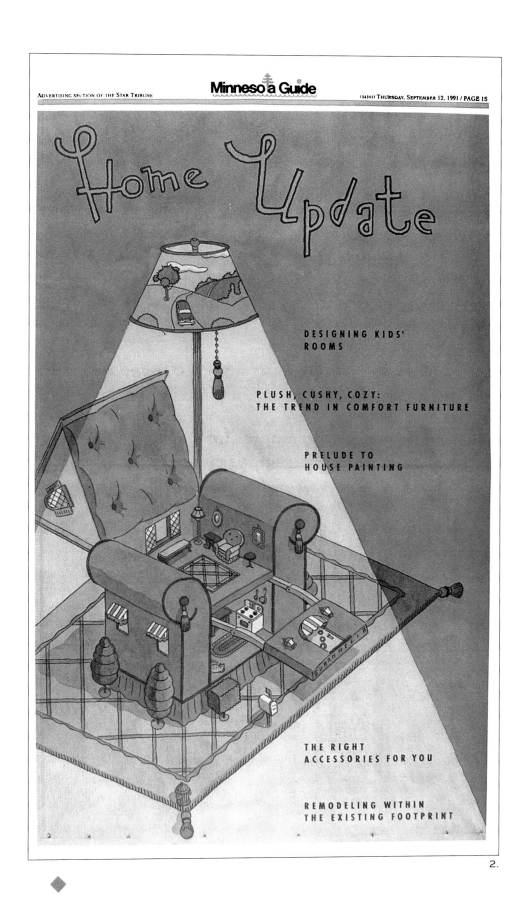

DESIGNING KIDS'
ROOMS

PLUSH, CUSHY, COZY:
THE TREND IN COMFORT FURNITURE

PRELUDE TO
HOUSE PAINTING

THE RIGHT
ACCESSORIES FOR YOU

REMODELING WITHIN
THE EXISTING FOOTPRINT

2.

Fan decks (1–4) and color reference manuals (5,6) for Pantone Matching System.®

DESIGN FIRM:

Pentagram Design, New York, New York

PARTNER/DESIGNER:

Woody Pirtle

CREATIVE DIRECTORS:

Woody Pirtle, Curt Dwyer

DESIGNER: Matt Heck

ILLUSTRATORS:

Matt Heck, Tim Lewis, Woody Pirtle, Anthony Russo, Erin Van Slyck

1.

2.

3.

4.

5.

6.

Promotional poster.

DESIGN FIRM:

Pentagram Design, New

York, New York

ART DIRECTOR:

Michael Bierut

PHOTOGRAPHER:

Reven T.C. Wurman

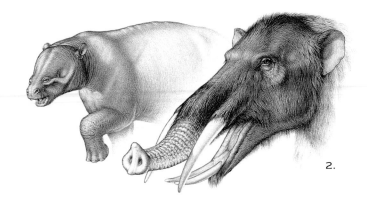

2.

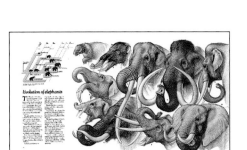

1.

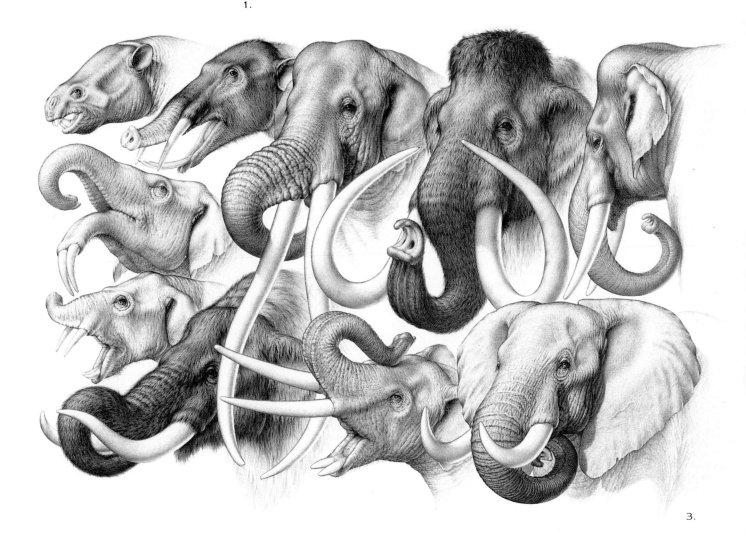

3.

Spreads and illustrations
from two articles in
National Geographic—one
on elephants (1-3) the
other on lyme disease (4).

DESIGN FIRM:
National Geographic
Magazine, Washington, DC
ART DIRECTOR:
Nicholas Kirilloff
ILLUSTRATORS:
Karel Havlicek (1-3),
Christopher A. Klein (4)

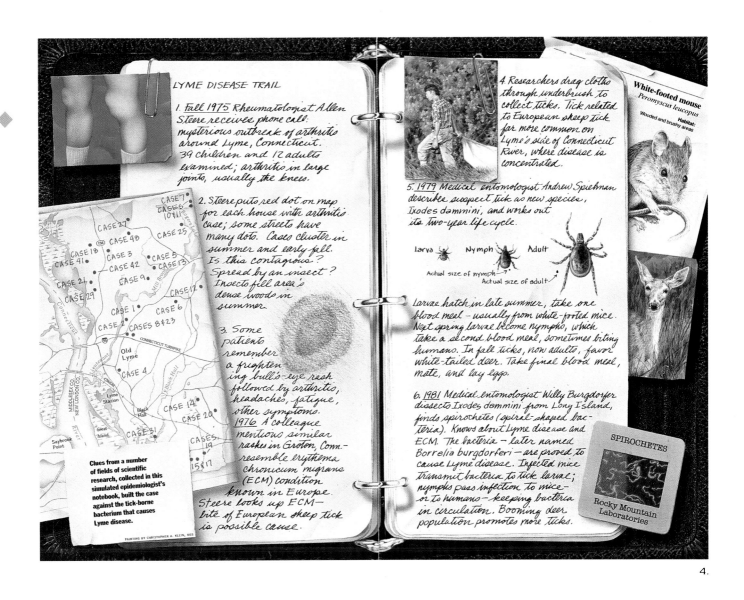

LYME DISEASE TRAIL

1. *Fall 1975* Rheumatologist Allen Steere receives phone call: mysterious outbreak of arthritis around Lyme, Connecticut. 39 children and 12 adults examined; arthritis in large joints, usually the knees.

2. Steere puts red dot on map for each house with arthritis case; some streets have many dots. Cases cluster in summer and early fall. Is this contagious? Spread by an insect? Insects fill area's dense woods in summer.

3. Some patients remember a frightening bull's-eye rash followed by arthritis, headaches, fatigue, other symptoms. 1976 A colleague mentions similar rashes in Groton, Conn.—resemble erythema chronicum migrans (ECM) condition known in Europe. Steere looks up ECM—bite of European sheep tick is possible cause.

Clues from a number of fields of scientific research, collected in this simulated epidemiologist's notebook, built the case against the tick-borne bacterium that causes Lyme disease.

PAINTING BY CHRISTOPHER A. KLEIN, NGS

4. Researchers drag cloths through underbrush to collect ticks. Tick related to European sheep tick far more common on Lyme's side of Connecticut River, where disease is concentrated.

5. *1979* Medical entomologist Andrew Spielman describes suspect tick as new species, Ixodes dammini, and works out its two-year life cycle.

Larva   Nymph   Adult

Actual size of nymph
Actual size of adult

Larvae hatch in late summer, take one blood meal—usually from white-footed mice. Next spring larvae become nymphs, which take a second blood meal, sometimes biting humans. In fall ticks, now adults, favor white-tailed deer. Take final blood meal, mate, and lay eggs.

6. *1981* Medical entomologist Willy Burgdorfer dissects Ixodes dammini from Long Island, finds spirochetes (spiral-shaped bacteria). Knows about Lyme disease and ECM. The bacteria—later named Borrelia burgdorferi—are proved to cause Lyme disease. Infected mice transmit bacteria to tick larvae; nymphs pass infection to mice—or to humans—keeping bacteria in circulation. Booming deer population promotes more ticks.

White-footed mouse
Peromyscus leucopus
Habitat:
Wooded and brushy areas

SPIROCHETES
Rocky Mountain Laboratories

4.

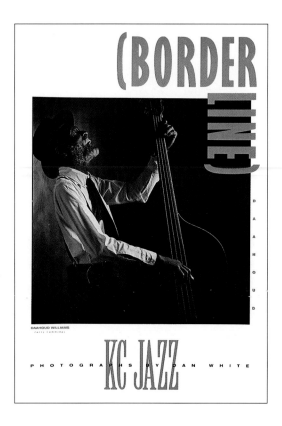

Cover and spread.

DESIGN FIRM: WRK Design,

Kansas City, Missouri

ART DIRECTOR/

DESIGNER: Debbie Robinson

PHOTOGRAPHER:

Dan White

Front and back covers,
spread and spot illustrations
from promotional booklet
for Macintosh training and
consulting business.

DESIGN FIRM: Miller Mauro
Group, Wilmington, Delaware

Miller Mauro Group (Advertising/Graphic Design/Macintosh Training & Consulting)

ART DIRECTORS:
Joe Mauro, Jon McPheeters
DESIGNER/ILLUSTRATOR:
Andy Cruz
PHOTOGRAPHERS:
Joe Mauro, Ruthea Miller
COPYWRITERS: Joe Mauro,
Rich Roat, Chris Vargas

Editorial spread.

DESIGN FIRM: Macworld,

San Francisco, California

ART DIRECTOR:

Joanne Hoffman

DESIGNER: Tim Johnson

ILLUSTRATOR: John Hersey

Listen
to your

history.

Columbia, Epic, Def Jam, RAL, Ruffhouse Ruthless, Word, Solar,
Orpheus and 40 Acres and A Mule
salute Black History. This month and every month.

Public-service ad
commemorating Black
History Month.
DESIGN FIRM: Sony Music,
New York, New York
ART DIRECTOR:
Nicky Lindeman
PHOTOGRAPHER:
Angela Fisher
COPYWRITER: Kim Greene

Ad campaign.

AGENCY: Brainstorm, Inc.,

Dallas , Texas

ART DIRECTORS:

Thomas Vasquez, Chuck

Johnson

DESIGNER:

Thomas Vasquez

PHOTOGRAPHER:

Neil Whitlock

COPYWRITER:

Chuck Johnson

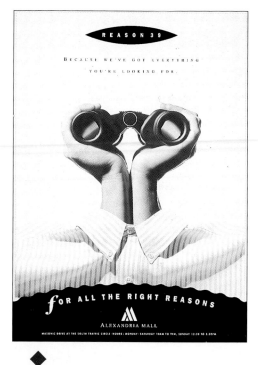

Marathon Shopping Centers Group

Series of postcards for sale.

DESIGN FIRM:

Gunnar Johnson,

Providence, Rhode Island

DESIGNER/ILLUSTRATOR:

Gunnar Johnson

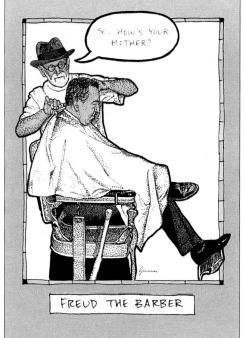

FREUD THE BARBER

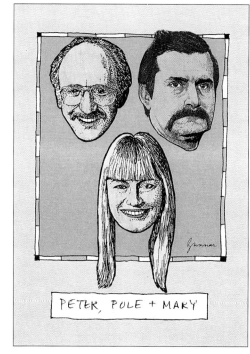

PETER, POLE + MARY

Recycled Paper Products, Inc. (Greeting Cards)

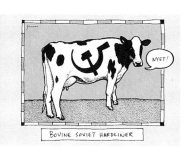

BOVINE SOVIET HARDLINER

DUMMY CORPORATION

DON KING CRAB

SALVADOR DALI PARTON

Poster for Gitanes.

DESIGN FIRM:

The Pushpin Group, Inc.,

New York, New York

ART DIRECTOR/

DESIGNER/ILLUSTRATOR:

Seymour Chwast

Recruitment poster sent to students accepted for admission who remained undecided.

DESIGN FIRM:

Tulane University Relations, New Orleans, Louisiana

ART DIRECTOR:

Tana Coman

DESIGNER: Jan Bertman

PHOTOGRAPHER:

Jerry Ward

ILLUSTRATOR:

Darryl White, YA/YA Inc.

COPYWRITER:

Mary Ann Travis

Promotional mailer.

DESIGN FIRM:

Fotheringham & Associates,

Salt Lake City, Utah

CREATIVE DIRECTOR/

COPYWRITER: Rod Miller

ART DIRECTOR/

DESIGNER/ILLUSTRATOR:

Randy Stroman

STS Production (Video Post-Production)

Build layer upon layer upon layer and never lose a generation.

Cover and spreads from
self-promotional brochure.
DESIGN FIRM:
The Pushpin Group, Inc.,
New York, New York
ART DIRECTOR:
Seymour Chwast
DESIGNER: Roxanne Slimak
PHOTOGRAPHER:
Jim Huibregtse

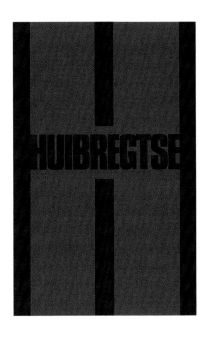

Record album cover.

DESIGN FIRM:

Kosh Brooks Design, Los

Angeles, California

ART DIRECTORS: Vartan,

Larry Brooks

DESIGNER: Larry Brooks

PHOTOGRAPHER:

Hiroyuki Arakawa

Promotional poster for an
AIGA exhibit.
DESIGN FIRM:
Michael Schwab Design,
Sausalito, California
DESIGNER/ILLUSTRATOR:
Michael Schwab

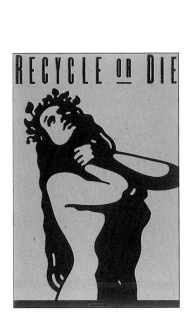

Cover and spreads from

1990 annual report.

DESIGN FIRM:

Pentagram Design, New

York, New York

PARTNER/DESIGNER:

Woody Pirtle

DESIGNER: Leslie Pirtle

ILLUSTRATOR:

Anthony Russo

PHOTOGRAPHER:

Ron Baxter Smith

TYPOGRAPHY:

Pastore de Ramphilis

Rampone

PRINTER: L.P. Thebault Co.

Northern Telecom (Telecommunications)

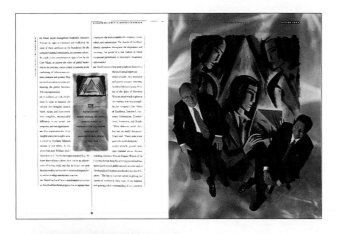

Illustrations and spread
from promotional brochure.
DESIGN FIRM:
Antista Design, Atlanta,
Georgia
ART DIRECTOR/
DESIGNER: Tom Antista
ILLUSTRATORS:
Dennis Mukia, Kevin
Newman

Flatland (Illustration for Design and Advertising)

1.

2.

Registration posters (1,2). Poster commemorating the 500th anniversary of Columbus' encounter with the Americas (3,4)—a calendar of each month's events was printed in the blank portion.

DESIGN FIRM:
BYU Graphics, Provo, Utah
ART DIRECTOR/
DESIGNER/ILLUSTRATOR:
McRay Magleby
SILKSCREENER:
Rory Robinson

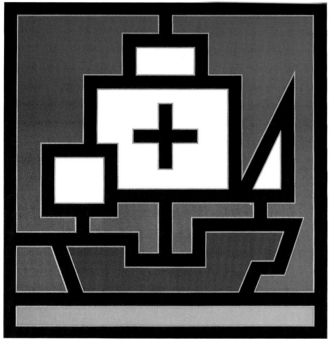

3.

4.

There Are Two Philosophies
For Cutting Corporate Travel Costs.

Choose your weapon. You can snip a little here, a little there, or you can call Southwest Airlines and cut airfares in a big way.

Southwest offers the lowest, everyday, unrestricted fares in the air for our frequent business travelers. And we don't penalize you for last minute changes in plans. Our unrestricted fares stay the same whether you purchase days in advance or at the gate.

Quite a difference from how business flyers are treated by our competition.

And we're different in other ways as well.

We've been in business for 20 years. Profitable for the last 18. And we're the only major airline that can say that.

If you are really serious about cutting travel costs, call the airline that is serious about helping you do it. **SOUTHWEST AIRLINES**

Ad.

AGENCY: Cramer-Krasselt,

Chicago, Illinois

CREATIVE DIRECTOR/

COPYWRITER:

Maureen Moore

ART DIRECTOR:

Doug Githens

PHOTOGRAPHER:

Charles Shotwell

Southwest Airlines

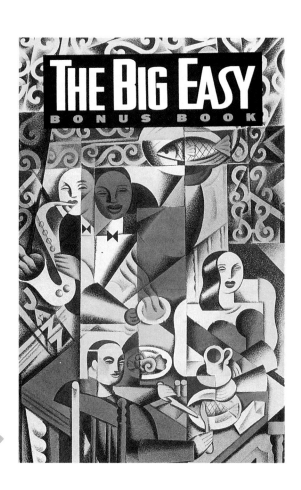

Front cover and complete

jacket of promotional

coupon book.

ILLUSTRATOR:

Mark Andresen, Metairie,

Louisiana

DESIGN FIRM:

Montgomery, Stire &

Erhardt

ART DIRECTOR/

DESIGNER: Phillip Collier

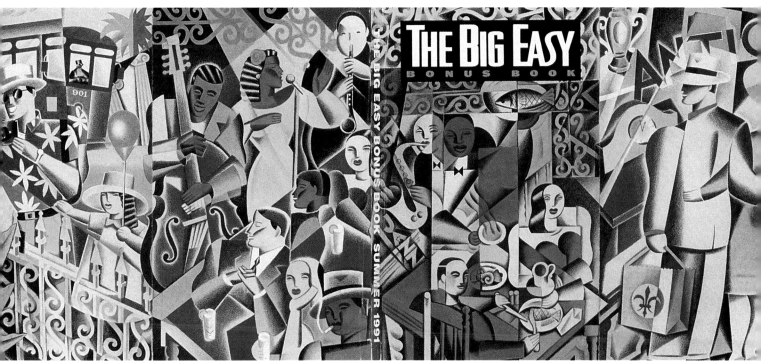

Graphic Ads

Promotional ad.

ILLUSTRATOR: Bill Mayer,

Decatur, Georgia

DESIGN FIRM:

Sullivan Haas Coyle

ART DIRECTOR:

Jerry Sullivan

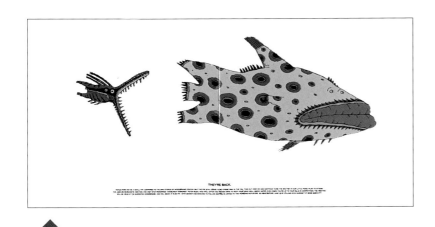

Promotional poster.

ILLUSTRATOR: Bill Mayer,

Decatur, Georgia

DESIGN FIRM: Adworks

ART DIRECTOR: Shirley Fee

Woodbridge Center (Shopping Malls)

Poster series.

DESIGN FIRM:

Ziff Marketing, New York,

New York

ART DIRECTOR:

Alane Gahagan

DESIGNER: Lori Littlehales

ILLUSTRATOR:

Wiktor Sadowski

Candy packaging.

DESIGN FIRM:

The Pushpin Group, Inc.,

New York, New York

ART DIRECTOR: Jim Burton

DESIGNER/ILLUSTRATOR:

Seymour Chwast

Kallir, Philips, Ross, Inc.

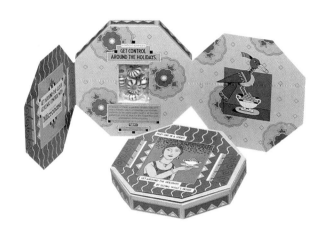

Joint promotional poster for a seminar at the University of Texas at El Paso and a meeting of the Graphic Arts Society of El Paso.

AGENCY:

Mithoff Advertising Inc., El Paso, Texas

ART DIRECTOR/ DESIGNER: Clive Cochran

ILLUSTRATOR:

Melissa Grimes

PRINTER:

Guynes Printing Company

SEPARATOR:

Sunset Colorgraphics

TYPOGRAPHER:

RJ Typesetters

Linc Cornell (Photography)

Self-promotional posters.

PHOTOGRAPHER:

Linc Cornell, South Natick,

Massachusetts

DESIGN FIRM:

PARTNERS & Simons

ART DIRECTORS:

Tom Simons, Nancy

LINC Cornell

LINC Cornell

LINC Cornell

Inside: Martha Smith interviews documentary-film maker Ken Burns

SUNDAY JOURNAL

MAGAZINE

June 23, 1991

Tropical diseases spread to New England

Cover and opening spread

of cover story.

DESIGN FIRM:

Providence Journal Sunday

Magazine, Providence,

Rhode Island

ART DIRECTOR:

Mick Cochran

DESIGNER:

Susan Huntemann

ILLUSTRATOR: Emily Lisker

FEVER and CHILLS

Tropical diseases are no longer a Third World phenomenon. As New Englanders increasingly travel the globe and as immigrants increasingly arrive from afar, doctors here are treating such ailments as malaria, bot-fly infestation, and leprosy.

STORY BY KAREN LEE ZINER

NAPSHOTS that Lynne Gould keeps of her friend Jack McClain show a balding, soft-bearded man with sparkling eyes and a yen for Bob Marley T-shirts. On her apartment walls, Gould keeps tokens of McClain's memory: leering African masks that he had collected. Two of McClain's cats, Gracie and Roger, roam the floors.

Jack McClain was an eclectic soul, Gould notes, with hurt in her eyes. "Very unconventional — probably the smartest person I've ever known. The funniest person I've ever known."

Christine Powell also knew McClain, for 22 years. She bore his daughter, now 15. Powell describes McClain as "an original."

He traveled extensively, to the West Coast, Jamaica, Haiti, and Europe. He accumulated folk art and other artifacts and four-leaf clovers, and he treasured everything his daughter wrote or drew. A baseball aficionado, McClain helped research and write *Baseballistics*, a book containing such information as brothers who both played professional baseball and

ILLUSTRATION BY
EMILY LISKER

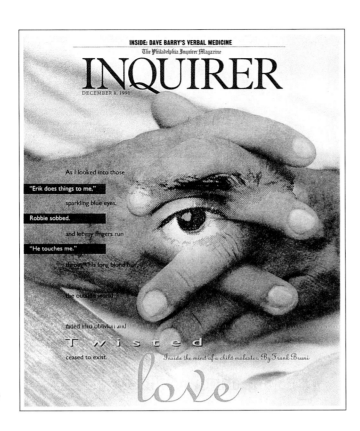

Cover and opening spread

of cover story.

DESIGN FIRM:

Philadelphia Inquirer

Magazine, Philadelphia,

Pennsylvania

ART DIRECTOR/

DESIGNER/ILLUSTRATOR:

Jessica Helfand

PHOTOGRAPHER:

William DeKay

WRITER: Frank Bruni

EDITOR: Suzanne L. Weston

HAND-COLORING:

J. Kyle Keener

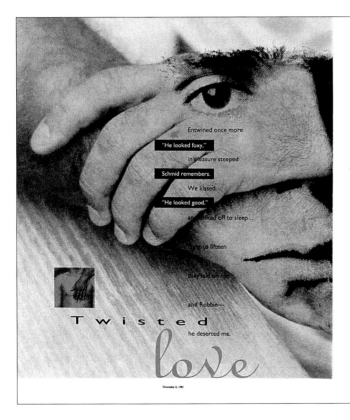

Ad campaign.

AGENCY: DDB Needham,

New York, New York

CREATIVE DIRECTOR:

Charlie Piccirillo

ART DIRECTOR/

DESIGNER:

Sharon Occhipinti

PHOTOGRAPHERS:

Stuart Heir (1), Nancy Ney

(3), Art Wolf (4), Raymond

Meier (5)

COPYWRITERS:

Susan Lieber (1), Doug

Raboy (3,5), Lisa Mayer (4)

Cream good enough for Colombian Coffee isn't exactly easy to find.

1.

Now that's flying first class.

2.

I see a man and a mule in your future.

3.

You can always tell a Colombian Coffee party by the way the crowd is dressed.

4.

Colombian Coffee

The perfect Sunday.

5.

78

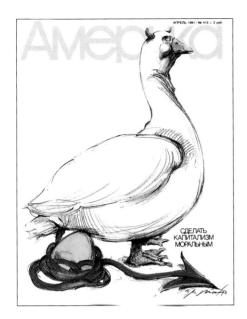

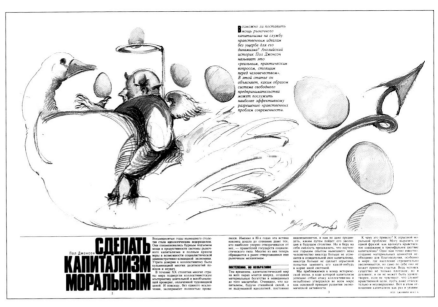

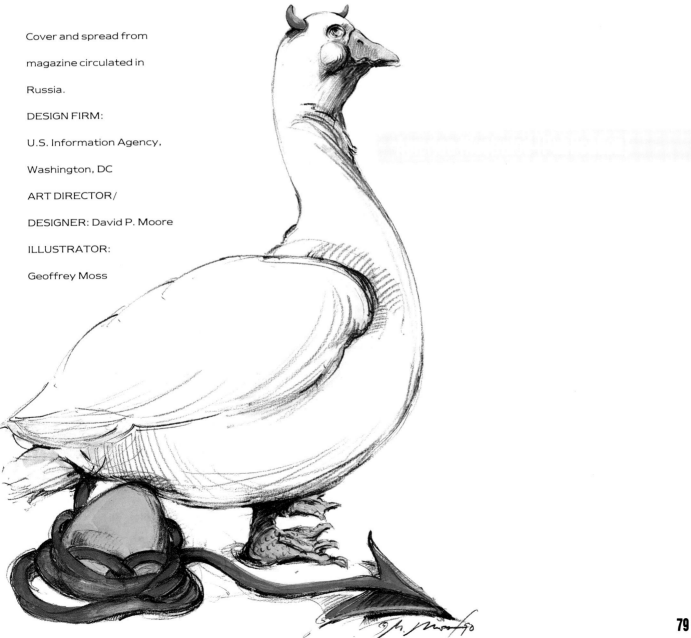

Cover and spread from

magazine circulated in

Russia.

DESIGN FIRM:

U.S. Information Agency,

Washington, DC

ART DIRECTOR/

DESIGNER: David P. Moore

ILLUSTRATOR:

Geoffrey Moss

Editorial spread.

DESIGN FIRM:

Hachette Publishing, Inc.,

New York, New York

ART DIRECTOR/

DESIGNER: Laura Sutcliffe

ILLUSTRATOR: David Lui

A DIFFERENT WORLD

The Auto Environment Challenges Audio Designers

THERE DEFINITELY IS more than one way to skin a cat—at least when it comes to designing audio components. Although the design objective—obtaining high-fidelity sound—for car and home equipment may be the same, the way to reach that goal is often quite different for each environment.

Indeed, what it all boils down to is the differences in the environments. The delivery of current is different in each—car electronics operate from an unstable, noisy, low-voltage DC source (the car's battery), while home gear operates from a relatively clean, stable, high-voltage AC source. The acoustical environment is different in each—not only is background noise greater in the car than at home, but the car itself is a closed box in which the listener sits in the "near field" of the speakers and is closer to some than to others. The thermal environment is different in each—car equipment must operate over a much wider temperature range than home equipment. And the mechanical environment is different in each—the physical size of components often is vital in the car, and installation becomes a problem, especially considering the shock and vibration that automotive gear is likely to experience.

To ascertain how these differences affect equipment design, we turned to four companies that make equipment for both environments: Denon for CD players, Audio Control for signal-processing and crossover design, Harman Kardon for power amps, and a/d/s/ for speakers.

BY ED FOSTER

Spot illustration and spread.

DESIGN FIRM:

Vermont Magazine, Bristol,

Vermont

ART DIRECTOR/

DESIGNER: Elaine Bradley

ILLUSTRATOR:

Greg Spalenka

Vermont Magazine

BADGER

A rich widow and an odd-job man bridge the gaps of culture and class

===== *Fiction by Priscilla Cypher* =====

TOO POOR TO BE CALLED A FARMER, BADGER WILLIAMS WAS AN odd-job man, nicknamed for his prominent chin, stocky build and stoical disposition. His life was as narrow and rock-hard as the Vermont valley in which he was born. He never had much, and had premonitions of even less.

Before the Depression, Badger's father had been in comfortable circumstances. But when the bank foreclosed on his thirty-acre farm, the old man's gumption faded and he died shortly after a heart spell. Badger and his wife Nellie went to live in a second-hand trailer on some land owned by Nellie's brother. Badger paid for use of the trailer by working occasionally on his brother-in-law's wood lots, getting out pulp and cord wood.

He accepted the change of fortune and in the 1940s hired out to Mrs. Harriet Winthrop down the valley toward Battle-

hill. He had worked off and on at her late husband's sawmill, enjoying the sour, clean smell of lumber.

But now he was surprised when she asked him to come into her kitchen. Hat in hand, he wiped his boots and stood running his eyes over the Staffordshire plates, lusterware and export china, thinking that Nellie would have said, "What's the good of fancy, a dish is a dish." Badger could feel Mrs. Winthrop watching him as she leaned her silver head forward saying, "Well, nothing's sure in this life but death and taxes! Now that Mr. Winthrop is gone, I have to support myself. Badger, I've decided to go into the antique business. It will give Larry something to do. We need your help."

Larry, Mrs. Winthrop's son, a sickly boy afflicted by headaches, had been a bookworm; he spent his time indoors

===== *Illustration by Greg Spalenka* =====

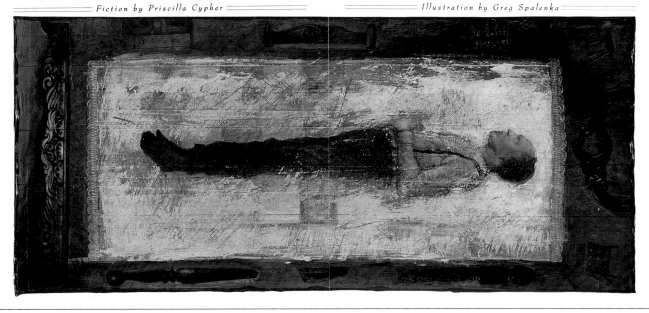

Ad campaign.

AGENCY: Young & Rubicam,

Chicago, Illinois

ART DIRECTOR:

Tom Shortlidge

PHOTOGRAPHER:

Brian Lanker

COPYWRITER: Mike Faems

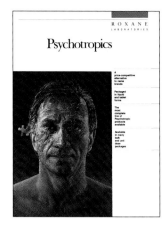

ROXANE
LABORATORIES

Psychotropics

A price-competitive alternative to name brands

Packaged in liquid and tablet forms

The most complete line of Psychotropic products available

Available in many bulk and unit dose packages

ROXANE
LABORATORIES

Oral
Schedule II
Narcotics

A price-competitive alternative to name brands

Packaged for ease of accountability

The most complete line of Schedule II products available

Available in many bulk and unit dose forms

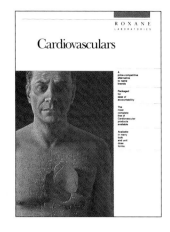

ROXANE
LABORATORIES

Cardiovasculars

A price-competitive alternative to name brands

Packaged for ease of accountability

The most complete line of Cardiovascular products available

Available in many bulk and unit dose forms

Series of product folders

used as sales tools.

DESIGN FIRM: Rickabaugh

Graphics, Gahanna, Ohio

ART DIRECTOR:

Eric Rickabaugh

DESIGNER: Mark Krumel

ILLUSTRATOR: John Martin

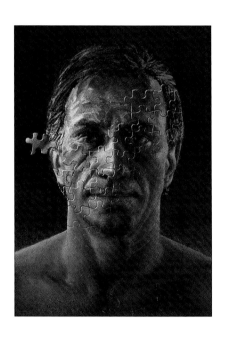

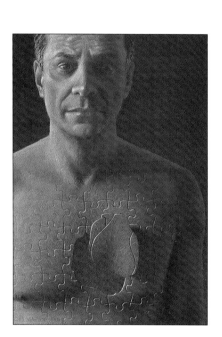

Roxanne Laboratories (Pharmaceutical Manufacturer)

THE METROPOLITAN OPERA SALUTES

MOZART 200

The Metropolitan Opera

Promotional poster.

DESIGN FIRM:

Milton Glaser, Inc., New

York, New York

ART DIRECTOR/

DESIGNER/ILLUSTRATOR:

Milton Glaser

Editorial spread.

DESIGN FIRM:

Whittle Communications, L.P.,

Knoxville, Tennessee

DESIGN DIRECTOR:

Bett McLean

ART DIRECTOR:

Tom Russell

DESIGNER:

Maureen Boneta

ILLUSTRATOR: Chris Gall

Best of Business Quarterly

Home Course in Religion

New Poems by **Gary Soto**

1.

Final book cover (1) and preliminary studies (2-4).

DESIGNER/ILLUSTRATOR: Alexander Laurant, Berkeley, California

DESIGN FIRM: Chronicle Books

ART DIRECTOR: Karen Pike

PHOTOGRAPHER: Alexander Laurant (collage elements)

2.

3.

4.

Promotional posters.

DESIGN FIRM:

QED Communications, Inc.,

Pittsburgh, Pennsylvania

ART DIRECTOR/

DESIGNER: Corey Glickman

ILLUSTRATOR:

Joseph Fiedler

TYPOGRAPHER:

Donald Antal

Magazine cover.

DESIGN FIRM:

Business Week

ART DIRECTOR:

Cynthia Friedman

ILLUSTRATOR: Bill Mayer,

Decatur, Georgia

Cover of FDA publication.

DESIGN FIRM:

Michael David Brown, Inc.,

Rockville, Maryland

ART DIRECTOR/

DESIGNER/ILLUSTRATOR:

Michael David Brown

You've got to stick your neck out to prosper.

Risk and reward travel side by side. Avoid the one, and the other will also pass you by.

But your choice of risk is critical. Some risk you want to take. Some, you don't.

Hide from risk and you hide from its rewards.

Helping you choose—and profit by your choice—is the strength of Bankers Trust. Our whole firm is dedicated to helping clients shed risk that can hurt them, assume risk by which they can profit.

We'll work with you day in, day out, to analyze your risk. We have the intellectual strength to make hard choices look easy. The market strength to turn strategy into reality. And the capital strength to keep every commitment we make.

Taking and managing risk is the mark of a leader. With Bankers Trust beside you, you'll truly be leading from strength.

◨ Bankers Trust   LEAD FROM STRENGTH.

Some risks are clearly visible. Others hide from sight.

The unexpected is the one thing you can always expect.

Risk. It isn't always where you expect it to be.

Suppose that overseas political upheaval thins out the flow of a raw material you can't do without. That's a risk Bankers Trust can help you contain.

Or suppose a natural disaster cripples your payments system. Again, with our merchant banking help, that risk can be dealt with.

Like every financial institution, we trade, arrange financing, close deals. But everything we do is done with an eye to helping you profit from risk.

Our greatest strength is putting all our skills to work at managing every kind of global risk.

Life can never be risk-free. Leadership isn't built on sure things. But with Bankers Trust behind you, you'll be leading from unparalleled strength.

◨ Bankers Trust   LEAD FROM STRENGTH.

Bankers Trust

Maybe you're building cars. Maybe you're building buildings. Between you and your corporate goals lies a complex set of risks.

Manage the risk, and you'll prosper. Ignore it, and you won't. Managing a business is almost wholly a matter of managing risk.

Risk surrounds almost everything worth having.

Here, Bankers Trust can help. Our whole enterprise is dedicated to helping clients shed risk that can hurt them. And assume risk by which they can profit.

We're not just talking traditional risk: currency, interest rates, commodity prices.

But if your market share is menaced by imports, we'll help you neutralize that threat. If your pension funds are lagging their liabilities, we'll help you fix that, too.

Surprised? Don't be. Our unique strength is managing virtually every type of global risk.

So go for the things worth having. Bankers Trust can help put them well within your grasp.

◨ Bankers Trust   LEAD FROM STRENGTH.

It's always tempting to focus on reward. But you've got to keep an eye on risk.

After all, there's no reward without it.

There's risk in energy prices. Which could make investing in, say, a transportation company hugely rewarding. Or sadly disappointing.

Risk. You have to look at it even when you don't want to.

There's risk in Latin America. And in Eastern Europe. But the opportunities there could be larger than those at home.

Everywhere you look, there's risk.

Managing risk—conventional and unconventional—is the single-minded mission of Bankers Trust. As merchant bankers, we've honed our ability to help you uncover risk, analyze it, take it or shed it, profit by it.

No firm is better equipped to help you see and deal with global risk. With Bankers Trust beside you, you

Ad campaign.

DESIGN FIRM:

Doremus & Co.

DESIGNER: Guy Marino

ILLUSTRATOR:

Brad Holland, New York,

New York

Magazine cover.

DESIGN FIRM:

Metropolis Magazine, New

York, New York

ART DIRECTORS:

Carl Lehmann-Haupt,

Nancy Cohen

PHOTOGRAPHER:

Kristine Larsen

HOMOSEXUALITY—NO WAY OUT?

by Jon Trott

ALITY—NO WAY OUT? HOMOSEXU

"I THINK THE CHRISTIAN COMMUNITY HAS TO TAKE RESPONSIBILITY FOR ANYTHING NEGATIVE IN ITS ATTITUDES TOWARDS HOMOSEXUAL PEOPLE."

Elizabeth Moberly and Tony Campolo Square off in the Gay Debate.

Cornerstone Magazine

Editorial spread.

DESIGN FIRM:

Cornerstone Graphics,

Chicago, Illinois

ART DIRECTOR:

Dick Randall

DESIGNER/ILLUSTRATOR:

Bruce Bitmead

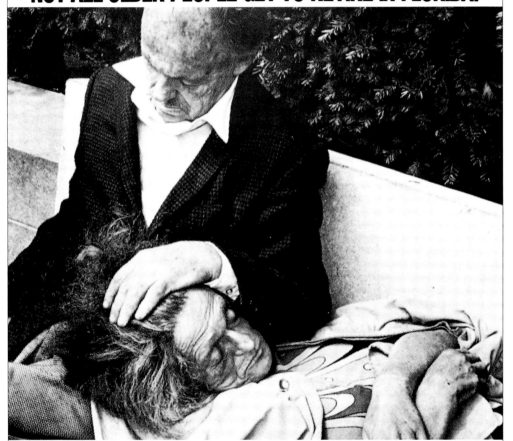

NOT ALL OLDER PEOPLE GET TO RETIRE IN FLORIDA.

The Elderly. Children At Risk. Families In Crisis. The Hungry And Homeless. AIDS Crisis Fund. Health And Rehabilitation. There's One Way To Help In Lots Of Ways.

THE UNITED WAY OF METROPOLITAN ATLANTA.

Promotional posters.

AGENCY: Fitzgerald & Co.,
Atlanta, Georgia

ART DIRECTOR: Kim Cable

PHOTOGRAPHERS:

James Conroy (Older

People), Bryan Morehead

(Expose Children)

COPYWRITER: Guy Lowe

Freeman Cosmetics Inc.

Skin care products

packaging.

DESIGN FIRM:

Peter J. Pataki Design,

Santa Monica, California

ART DIRECTOR/

DESIGNER/ILLUSTRATOR:

Peter J. Pataki

TYPOGRAPHER:

Kathleen Kaiser

CD packaging.

DESIGN FIRM:

Morla Design, San Francisco,

California

ART DIRECTOR:

Jennifer Morla

DESIGNERS: Jennifer Morla,

Jeanette Aramburu

PHOTOGRAPHER:

Bybee Studios

From Vietnam to Jim Morrison, OLIVER STONE keeps telling America his personal history. Does he tell it like it was?

60s something

HEARD THE FIRST DOORS ALBUM ON ACID IN VIETNAM," OLIVER Stone says, flashing his famous gap-toothed grin. "I liked their apocalyptic vision, their sense of dread, their eroticism." LSD in a rock 'n' roll war. Combat psychedelics. I can't imagine anything more hellish. Trips were strange and overpowering enough on the home front. Why risk chemically induced paranoia in the jungle? Why enhance the surreal violence of the killing fields? "It was crazy," answers the forty-four-year-old director. "But so was the war."

Stone sits behind an empty desk, sipping bottled water in a starkly anonymous room in a west Los Angeles sound studio. The walls are bare. Reels of 35-mm film in silver cans litter the floor. The air conditioner hisses. It's ice cold. He looks pale and drawn—a man who has spent too many hours in

by stephen talbot

Illustration by Philip Burke

1.

Editorial spreads.

DESIGN FIRM:

Mother Jones Magazine,

San Francisco, California

ART DIRECTOR:

Kerry Tremain

DESIGNERS:

Marsha Sessa (1), Kerry

Tremain (2)

ILLUSTRATORS:

Philip Burke (1), Anita

Kunz (2)

SECRET
TOUCHES

A father's search for the man

who molested his son—and what

he discovers about himself.

THREE YEARS AGO, I RETURNED HOME from a long road trip several days ahead of schedule. For weeks I'd been looking forward to being home with my family. Naturally, I was a little disappointed when my wife, Lisa,* told me our son was spending the night with Tim. A teacher's aide at our town's one-room country schoolhouse, Tim had befriended Christopher, who was seven at the time.

I'd never met Tim, but Lisa had, and, like most of the members of our small, close-knit community, she found him to be open, friendly, and intelligent. He'd become the baby-sitter of choice among our friends.

Still, I was uneasy, though I couldn't quite put words to it. I wrote it off to my big-city upbringing. "You're too trusting, Lisa," I grumbled. "Why couldn't Chris simply meet Tim in the morning?"

Lisa argued that I was gone so much, and Chris really seemed to be in need of Tim's companionship just then. They weren't expecting me to return for almost a week. It wasn't fair to make Chris wait. Besides, two of Chris's friends would also be spending the night at Tim's. Chris would be all right. Smile. Kiss. Melt.

The fact was, Tim was irresistible, and he was there when I wasn't. He took Chris mountain biking after school, taught him funny songs, bought him soda pops. Best of all, Tim let Chris sit on his lap and steer his Volvo wagon on the back roads.

And as I came to find out, he sexually molested my son.

The weeks and months that followed this revelation were, as one would expect, an emotionally hellish time for our family. But we never in our wildest dreams could have imagined the bureaucratic nightmare we would experience at the

*All names in this story have been changed. The author is a *Mother Jones* contributor who prefers to remain anonymous.*

46 MOTHER JONES/SEPT./OCT. 1991

hands of the authorities. Nor could I have known that before I would ever be of any real help to my son, I would have to face up to a long-buried secret of my own.

I'D ONLY BEEN HOME A FEW WEEKS WHEN I BEGAN TO NOTICE that Chris was acting more than "a little moody," which is how his teacher had described his behavior of late. I asked Chris if Tim, with whom he was spending more and more time, was doing anything that made him feel uncomfortable. He shrugged.

It wasn't like Chris. As a family we've always been very close. We lived Chris's earliest years in tents and funky one-room cabins in the mountains of the Pacific Northwest, hiking, climbing, hunting, fishing, gathering food, watching. When we could tear ourselves away from the landscape, I was an aspiring novelist, Lisa a painter.

Chris, not used to having other kids around much, wasn't the least shy with grown-ups, and when he couldn't convince us all to join him on a walkabout, he'd join us in conversation. By the time he was ready to start school, there was little he couldn't, or wouldn't, talk about. Which is why, when I asked him about his relationship with Tim, I found his shrug discomfiting.

Lisa thought Chris was just being hard on me for being gone so much over the past year. "He really depends on you," she said, "and he feels left out. You're going off and having adventures without him, now that he's in school." It was get-backs, Lisa said. Nothing a little time together wouldn't heal.

When I finally met Tim, at a community volleyball game,

Illustrations by Anita Kunz

2.

Transit shelter poster.

DESIGN FIRM:

LaMaster Farmer Et Al,

Minneapolis, Minnesota

ART DIRECTOR:

John Walker

PHOTOGRAPHER:

Rick Dublin

COPYWRITER: Jo Marshall

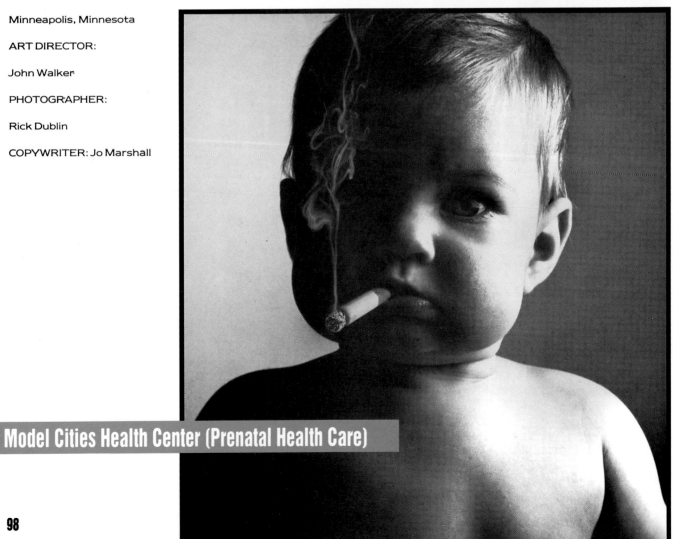

Model Cities Health Center (Prenatal Health Care)

Self-promotional booklet.

DESIGN FIRM: Philip Wende,

Canton, Georgia

DESIGNER/ILLUSTRATOR:

Philip Wende

Philip Wende (Graphic Design/Illustration)

Thoughtful Drawings by Philip Wende 404 479-5273

Cover (2), spreads (1,3,4) and photo (5) from capabilities brochure.

DESIGN FIRM:

The Kuester Group, Minneapolis, Minnesota

ART DIRECTORS:

Kevin B. Kuester, Brent Marmo

DESIGNER: Tim Sauer

PHOTOGRAPHERS:

Joe Paczkowski, Cheryl Rossum

COPYWRITER:

David Forney

SUITS: Steve Beaudry

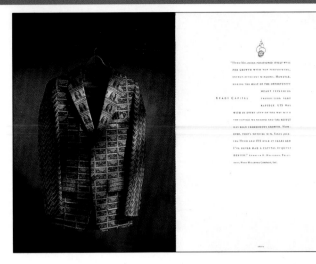

1.

2.

3.

4.

5.

Jim Ales Design (Graphic Design/Illustration)

Self promotion piece.

DESIGN FIRM:

Jim Ales Design, San

Francisco, California

ART DIRECTOR/

DESIGNER/ILLUSTRATOR:

Jim Ales

DESIGNER: Rick Roese

PHOTOGRAPHER:

Jeffery Newbury

COPYWRITER: Julie Page

Cover of special section.

DESIGN FIRM:

CMP Publications/Business

Travel News, Manhasset,

New York

ART DIRECTOR:

Teresa M. Carboni

ILLUSTRATOR: Terry Hoff

Cover of Orlando Sentinel
Sunday magazine.

DESIGN FIRM:

Florida Magazine, Orlando,
Florida

ART DIRECTOR/
DESIGNER:

Santa Choplin Bogdon

ILLUSTRATOR: Gene Greif

THE ORLANDO SENTINEL FEBRUARY 3, 1991

Florida

THE SEA IS COMING!
THE SEA IS COMING!
AND FLORIDA'S IN THE WAY

PLUS : BOB MORRIS ON BAD TASTE

Spot photos (1), and front (2) and back (3) covers of promotional CD.

DESIGN FIRM:

Warner Bros. Records, Burbank, California

ART DIRECTORS: Jeff Gold, Kim Champagne

DESIGNER:

Kim Champagne

PHOTOGRAPHER:

Enrique Badulescu

1.

2.

9 26644-2

3.

Editorial spread.

DESIGN FIRM:

Investment Vision, Boston,

Massachusetts

ART DIRECTOR/

DESIGNER: Carol Layton

ILLUSTRATOR: Bill Nelson

Investment Vision Magazine

DeWalt & Associates

Ad for artist's representative.

AGENCY:

Laughlin/Constable, Inc.,

Milwaukee, Wisconsin

CREATIVE DIRECTOR:

John Constable

ART DIRECTOR:

Scotti Larson

COPYWRITER: Brad Berg

PHOTOGRAPHER:

Dave Gilo

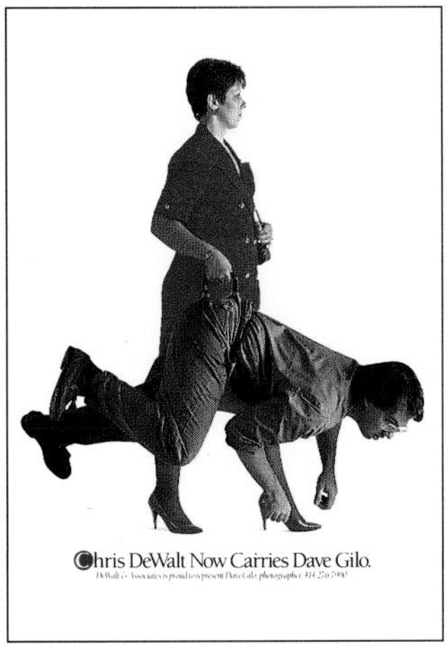
Chris DeWalt Now Carries Dave Gilo.

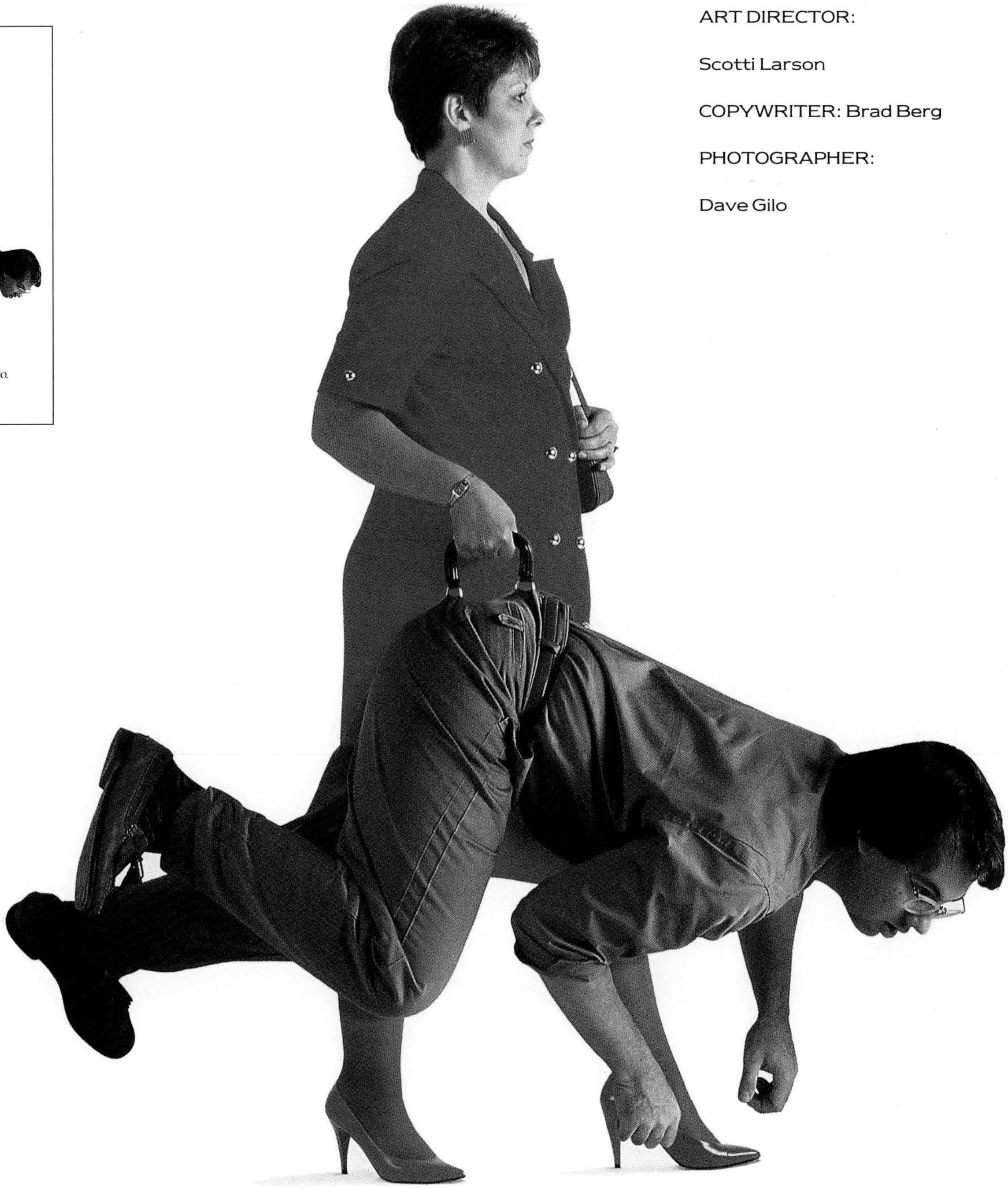

Ad campaign.

AGENCY:

Laughlin/Constable, Inc.,

Milwaukee, Wisconsin

CREATIVE DIRECTORS:

Ken Butts, Kirk Ruhnke

ART DIRECTOR: Ken Butts

DESIGNER: Todd Brei (logo)

PHOTOGRAPHER: Ken Reid

COPYWRITER: Kirk Ruhnke

Book cover.

DESIGN FIRM: Henry Holt,

New York, New York

ART DIRECTOR/

DESIGNER: Raquel Jaramillo

ILLUSTRATOR:

James Steinberg

Poster promoting the
association's annual golf
tournament.
DESIGN FIRM:
Sullivan Perkins, Dallas,
Texas
ART DIRECTOR:
Ron Sullivan
DESIGNER/ILLUSTRATOR:
Jon Flaming

Ad campaign.

DESIGN FIRM:

Dawson & Company, Grand

Rapids, Michigan

ART DIRECTOR/

DESIGNER:

Thomson Dawson

PHOTOGRAPHER:

Bernard Cohen

Announcement poster (1), reminder card (2), winner notification (3) and illustration (4) for the 8th International Awards of Excellence.

DESIGN FIRM:

Esprit Communications, Costa Mesa, California

ART DIRECTOR:

Coen Van de Poll

ILLUSTRATORS:

Kevin Short, Ken Jacobson

COPYWRITERS:

Alan Proctor, Mark Cacciatore

PRODUCTION MANAGER:

Diedre Nelson

ACCOUNT MANAGER:

Martha Higgins

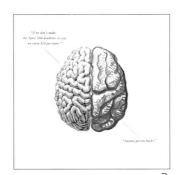

THE BEST WORK FROM
BOTH HEMISPHERES.

1.

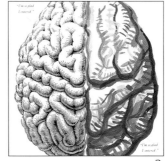

2.

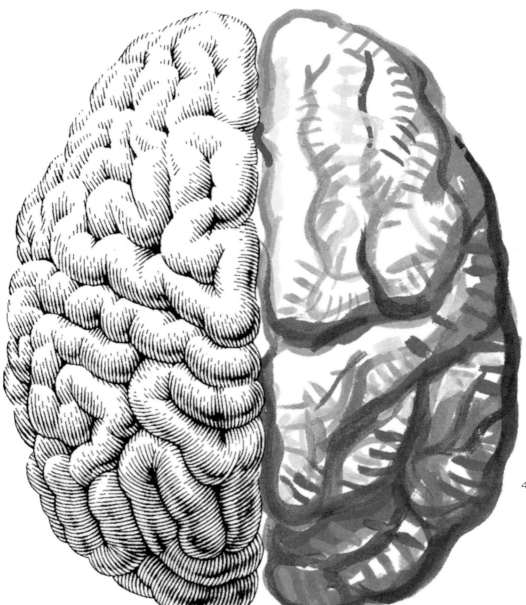

3.

4.

Ad campaign.

AGENCY:

Loeffler Ketchum Mountjoy,

Charlotte, North Carolina

ART DIRECTOR:

Tom Routson

PHOTOGRAPHER:

Steve Murray

COPYWRITER: Steve Skibba

Here in North Carolina, autumn guests are given a colorful reception. One that could make you forget the mountains on our western border are known as the Blue Ridge. Brilliant reds. Lush auburns. Rich golds. The leaves on over a hundred species of

harvest festivals, held every year for as long as anyone can remember, and the glow of the setting sun on beaches inhabited not by high rise hotels, but by sea birds and shells. It's a land awash in local color. And as you wind your way through the state

WHEN WE ROLL OUT THE RED CARPET, IT'S 250 MILES LONG.

trees blend into miles and miles of crimson forests. Forests unchanged since the days when Daniel Boone first explored them. But then, you'll soon discover many things in North Carolina remain unchanged, as you do a little exploring of your own.

You'll see the firing of centuries-old pottery kilns. You'll see the vibrant panels of quilts, still stitched by patient hands instead of machines. You'll see the golden wanes of our

Sir Walter Raleigh and the first English colonists called home, we think you'll find the term red carpet is very much appropriate. NORTH CAROLINA

You see, in North Carolina, hospitality is more than just a word. It's a way of life. So this fall, why not join us here, where the event of the season is the season itself. After all, nature will be going to some pretty great lengths to welcome you. And we will too.

North Carolina Travel & Tourism

Cross the inland waterway to North Carolina's barrier islands, and you leave more than just the mainland behind. Everyday concerns vanish. Cares evaporate. Stress fades. The tranquil shores where English explorers first planted their flag are now the

all, where the Wright brothers' career took off. As for sightseeing, it would be pretty hard to miss our lighthouses, or Jockey's Ridge, the largest sand dune on the east coast. But if you simply want to relax on the sand with a good book, feel free. North

THESE WATERS SEPARATE OUR ISLANDS FROM THE COAST. AND YOU FROM YOUR CARES.

perfect place to plant a beach umbrella. The secluded coves where Blackbeard and his pirates once sought refuge can be your sanctuary too. Even the names of the islands and villages — Ocracoke, Nags Head, Sneads Ferry — seem to conjure up a more peaceful era.

Of course, not everything here will remind you of days gone by. You can always unwind with such modern pastimes as hang gliding and wind surfing. This is, after

Carolina boasts a mild climate year round. And, as anyone who's ever been here can attest, even our public beaches are still very private. NORTH CAROLINA

When you're ready to put a little distance between yourself and the distractions of everyday life, come spend some time with us off the North Carolina coast. Although you just might find it hard to separate yourself from here when it's time to leave.

Poster distributed to car
dealers nationwide
promoting a new speaker
system.

AGENCY:

Young & Laramore,

Indianapolis, Indiana

CREATIVE DIRECTORS:

David Young, Jeff Laramore

ART DIRECTOR:

Mark Bradley

PHOTOGRAPHER:

Drew Endicott

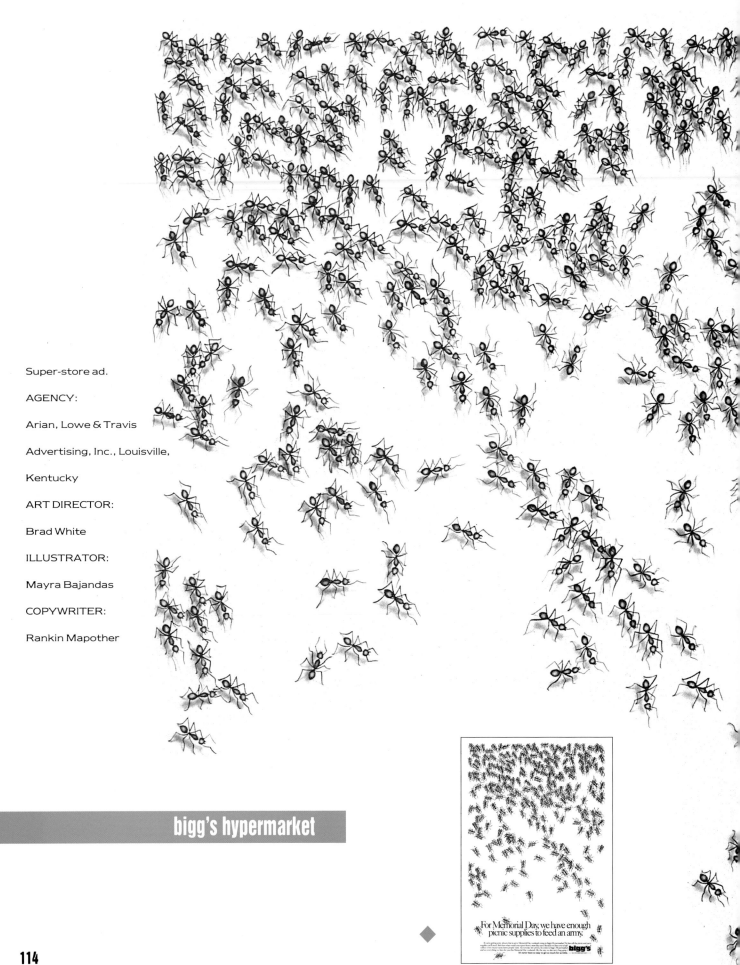

Super-store ad.

AGENCY:

Arian, Lowe & Travis

Advertising, Inc., Louisville,

Kentucky

ART DIRECTOR:

Brad White

ILLUSTRATOR:

Mayra Bajandas

COPYWRITER:

Rankin Mapother

bigg's hypermarket

For Memorial Day, we have enough
picnic supplies to feed an army.

114

Book jacket.

DESIGN FIRM:

Acme Design Company,

Wichita, Kansas

ART DIRECTOR:

John Baxter

ILLUSTRATOR:

Jacqui Morgan

WATERMARK PRESS $20.⁰⁰

"George Stanley has let the cat out of the bag about Kansas fishing secrets."
Honorable Mike Hayden
Assistant Secretary of the Interior
for Fish, Wildlife, and Parks

"George Stanley has written the definitive book on fishing in Kansas.
Its well-designed pages are filled with inside track information which will delight
anglers and make fish nervous. It's a keeper."
Steve Harper
Outdoors Writer, *The Wichita Eagle*

"George Stanley's writing reads easy, like water down a lazy Flint Hills stream.
And typical of his work, exhaustive research gives readers an enormous amount of useful
information. Even lifelong Kansas anglers will enjoy and learn from this book."
Mike Miller
Editor, *Kansas Wildlife and Parks*

Cover illustration by Jacqui Morgan

Watermark Guide to Fishing in Kansas ❧ George Stanley ❧ Watermark

Watermark Guide to Fishing in Kansas

A celebration of sportfishing that includes:
How, where and when to find bass, walleye,
stripers, wipers and other favorite fish
species right here in
Kansas. Detailed
maps of all major
reservoirs. A guide
to Kansas streams and public access points.
Tips for gaining access to hot spots on
private property.

ISBN 0-922820-14-7

52000>

9 780922 820146

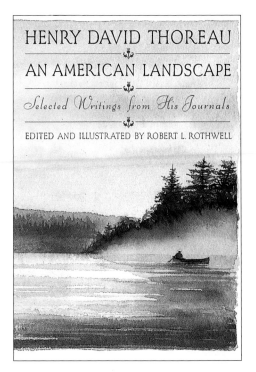

Book cover.

DESIGN FIRM:

Wendell Minor Design,

Washington, Connecticut

ART DIRECTOR:

Susan Newman

DESIGNER/ILLUSTRATOR:

Wendell Minor

Covers of annual magazine
on international photography
published by Minolta.

DESIGN FIRM:

Bechlen/Gonzalez, Inc.,

Honolulu, Hawaii

ART DIRECTOR/

DESIGNER: Fred Bechlen

PHOTOGRAPHERS:

Rokuo Kawakami (1), Uwe
Ommer (2), Ines E. Roberts
(3), Freeman Patterson (4)

EDITOR: Richard V. Bryant

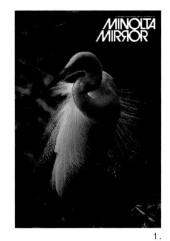

1.

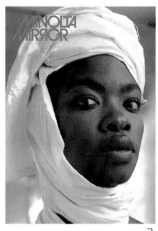

2.

Minolta Camera Company, Ltd.

3.

4.

Front page (1) of 'Insight'—

political commentary

section of Sunday edition.

Black plate of pen-and-ink

drawing (2) and watercolor

overlay (3).

DESIGNER/ILLUSTRATOR:

Don Asmussen, Ypsilanti,

Michigan

ART DIRECTOR:

Rick Wakely

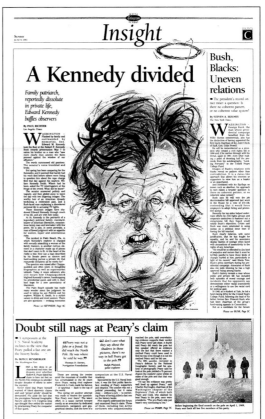

1.

2.

3.

1.

2.

Poster commemorating the

opening of the Gorilla

Tropics exhibit (4). Designs

(1–3) used as reference.

ILLUSTRATOR: Tracy Sabin,

San Diego, California

DESIGN FIRM:

Bodney Siedler Design

ART DIRECTOR/

DESIGNER: Brenda Bodney

3.

4.

Ad for Alfa Romeo 164.

AGENCY: Ross Roy, Inc.,

Bloomfield Hills, Michigan

ART DIRECTOR:

Jack Frakes

ILLUSTRATOR:

Camille Przewodek

COPYWRITER:

Lance Aldrich

IMPRESSIONS OF THE ALFA ROMEO 164:

"At the heart of the car is Alfa's familiar all-aluminum 3-liter V-6, a power plant that puts to shame any 6-cylinder manufactured in this country. If awards were given for smoothness, this engine would rank right up there with whipped cream, silk sheets and a baby's derriere."

C. Van Tune
Motor Trend
Artist: Camille Przewodek

Among the world's most revered automakers, probably none understands the relationship between car and driver better than Alfa Romeo. The 3.0-liter V-6 powered ABS-equipped 164S high performance luxury sedan is testimony to that. And with its all-inclusive Alfa Romeo Assurance Program,* it is clear that we also understand the relationship between car and owner.

*For 3 years or 36,000 miles, whichever comes first. See your dealer for details and a copy of the plan.
©1991 Alfa Romeo Distributors of North America.

Alfa Romeo.
The legendary marque of high performance.

To find out more about the Alfa Romeo 164 and how to obtain a free 20" x 24" print of the illustration at left, while supplies last, call
1-800-245-ALFA.

Promotional poster.

DESIGN FIRM:

Delessert & Marshall,

Lakeville, Connecticut

ART DIRECTOR:

Rita Marshall

ILLUSTRATOR:

Etienne Delessert

Promotional ad for the book
Circle of Life, sponsored and
published by Kodak.
PHOTOGRAPHER:
Jamey Stillings, Rochester,
New York
DESIGN FIRM:
Rumrill-Hoyt, Inc.
ART DIRECTOR: Jane Weeks

CREATING A BEAUTIFUL TAPESTRY REQUIRES THE FINEST MATERIALS.

THAT'S WHY THE PHOTOGRAPHERS WHOSE IMAGES ENRICH THE CIRCLE OF LIFE USED KODAK PROFESSIONAL FILM. IT'S THE ONE THREAD THAT BINDS TOGETHER THE DIVERSE RITUALS IN THIS REVEALING TABLEAU. WE ARE PROUD TO SPONSOR THIS BOOK AND TRAVELING EXHIBITION AS PART OF OUR ONGOING COMMITMENT TO LEADERSHIP IN PHOTOGRAPHIC PUBLISHING AND OF OUR SUPPORT OF PHOTOGRAPHIC PROJECTS THAT CONTRIBUTE TO AN EXPANDED AWARENESS OF OUR OWN LIVES AND THOSE OF OUR NEIGHBORS IN THE GLOBAL VILLAGE.

PROFESSIONAL PHOTOGRAPHY DIVISION

Eastman Kodak Company

Ad campaign.

DESIGN FIRM:

Javier Romero Design, Inc.,

New York, New York

ART DIRECTORS:

David Nathanson, Javier

Romero

DESIGNER: Javier Romero

ILLUSTRATORS:

Gary Saint Clare, Martin

Fitzpatrick, Javier Romero

PHOTOGRAPHER: Bo Hylen

"European touring sedan." Three little words that conjure up serious driving pleasure along with some very serious car payments. Not so with the Volkswagen Passat. It's the perfect balance of German suspension and handling in a car with 16 valves of hardened steel and 4-wheel disc brakes, all at a price that's not too heady. It's also the perfect combination of thoughtful features such as air conditioning, height adjustable steering column, front and rear adjustable seats— all standard. So look into the Passat. Experience Fahrvergnügen® and you'll come out saying, "Nobody, but nobody, can drive my Passat but me." FAHRVERGNÜGEN. IT'S WHAT MAKES A CAR A VOLKSWAGEN.

For details, call 1-800-444-VWUS

© 1991 Volkswagen

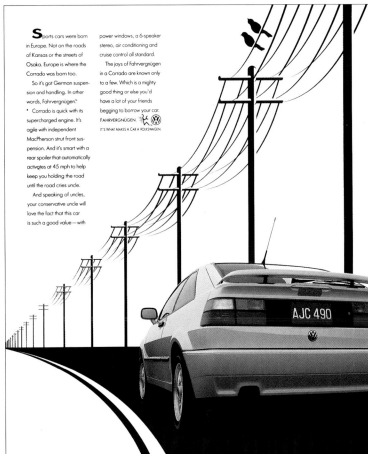

Sports cars were born in Europe. Not on the roads of Kansas or the streets of Osaka. Europe is where the Corrado was born too.

So it's got German suspension and handling. In other words, Fahrvergnügen.®

Corrado is quick with its supercharged engine. It's agile with independent MacPherson strut front suspension. And it's smart with a rear spoiler that automatically activates at 45 mph to help keep you holding the road until the road cries uncle.

And speaking of uncles, your conservative uncle will love the fact that this car is such a good value — with power windows, a 6-speaker stereo, air conditioning and cruise control all standard.

The joys of Fahrvergnügen in a Corrado are known only to a few. Which is a mighty good thing or else you'd have a lot of your friends begging to borrow your car. FAHRVERGNÜGEN. IT'S WHAT MAKES A CAR A VOLKSWAGEN.

Cover of a weekly tourism magazine promoting the week-long Rose Festival.

DESIGN FIRM:
Nancy Davis Design & Illustration, Portland, Oregon

ART DIRECTOR/ DESIGNER/ILLUSTRATOR:
Nancy Davis

Cover of Los Angeles Times

Sunday supplement.

ART DIRECTOR:

Nancy Duckworth/Los

Angeles Times Magazine,

Los Angeles, California

ILLUSTRATOR:

Josh Gosfield

WOMEN IN UNDERWEAR
much ado about little nothings

fiction By STEPHEN WOLF

EARLY SATURDAY NIGHT, Laura left her apartment to meet her lover, wearing the satin floral-print bra-and-panty set he had given her for Christmas. She had received a set in black silk for her birthday, a red camisole for Valentine's Day and numerous pairs of panties in cotton, satin and silk for no special reason, simply for his own delight in giving her lingerie. That her husband, too, would take pleasure from these gifts troubled her lover less than the possibility that other lingerie she wore might be gifts from another lover.

"And who gave you these little things?" he once had asked, his suspicion over her white-lace bra and panties momentarily greater than his arousal.

"I buy my own lingerie," she had replied, and he wondered if her husband had ever received the same answer to a similar question.

For 25 years, Eva had thought her breasts were too small. The fact that most women her age had breasts already sagging gave her no comfort. She wouldn't mind a little sag, but her breasts remained as perky and small as an adolescent's. She had blamed her mother for this misfortune and had spent her girlhood terribly self-conscious about what she considered a deformity, developing a mild case of round-shoulderedness in an attempt to hide what she did not have. Believing that boys desired only girls with large breasts, Eva was certain boys wanted nothing from her.

Eventually she met and fell in love with a man who thought himself too short. She would tell him that she liked being the same height as her lover because she felt equal, and he, in turn, gave elaborate, extensive attention to her breasts, which were very responsive. Although Eva and he each knew of the other's weakness, they never used this knowledge against each other, even in their worst arguments. He eventually left her for a shorter woman with, to Eva's relief, unremarkable breasts, and Eva regretted losing him as much from love as from fear at

114

PAINTINGS BY LARRY RIVERS

1.

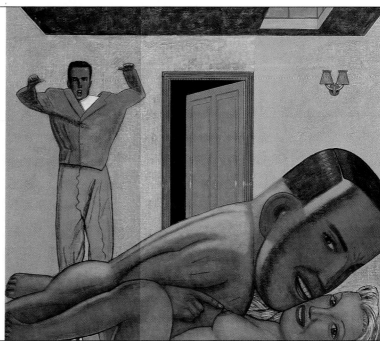

MY LIFE WITH JOANNE CHRISTIANSEN

"you'll walk in and he'll be bouncing on top of her, and she'll be screaming, 'oh, honey, you're so much more of a ma-yun than my husband'"

fiction By MARK ALPERT

HER NAME will be Joanne Christiansen. You'll meet her while you're driving your Trans Am through New Hampshire or Pennsylvania or Idaho, someplace rural. She'll be the type of girl who's impressed by a Trans Am. She'll walk over to you while you're stopped at a traffic light and she'll say, 'Hey, there, I like your car.' You'll try to strike a macho pose behind the steering wheel. Then she'll say, 'Yeah, it looks like a fast piece of equipment.' You'll say, 'I got some other equipment that's fast, too,' and she'll say, 'Oh, really?' But (continued on page 145)

100

PAINTING BY PAT ANDREA

2.

126

Editorial spreads.

DESIGN FIRM: Playboy,

Chicago, Illinois

ART DIRECTOR:

Tom Staebler

DESIGNERS: Kerig Pope

(1,2,4), Len Willis (3)

ILLUSTRATORS:

Larry Rivers (1), Pat

Andrea (2), Guy Billout (3),

Mel Odom (4)

gay bashing
is out of the closet. again

article By Nat Hentoff

A Case
of Loathing

RON JOHNSON, a waiter in Georgetown, was walking home one night through a park and passed an area known as a contact place for homosexuals. Suddenly, he was surrounded.

"They came out of the shadows," Johnson told *The Washington Post.* "They weren't waiting for me, just for someone." Someone gay. Beaten with baseball bats. Johnson didn't fully recover physically for months. His fingers were smashed and his arm and shoulder were broken in three places. It will be much longer before he will be able to control the memories of that ambush. He can no longer stand being alone in the dark, his windows are always locked and in his nightmares—always the same—he is brutally beaten. It is always the same nightmare.

Three 18-year-olds were arrested for the assault. One of them, Mark Hyder, explained that he and his friends had gone to the park that night specifically looking for gays to beat up. "I have a hatred for gays," Hyder said.

Johnson is one of a rising number of gays throughout the country who are considered fair game by roving bands of brutal homophobes. It is the conventional wisdom that the most vicious hate crimes are racist, but the mounting evidence indicates that violence against gays is more ferocious

3.

big
TROUBLE
IN
LITTLE SAIGON

in orange county, of all places,
the children of vietnam's
boat people roam our streets
in gangs, living a life of fast
cars, easy violence and
terrifying freedom

article By JIM GOAD

THE HEAD of the Asian gang unit pops a video cassette into his police-issue VCR. The screen erupts. In slo-mo black and white, showers of smoke and glass spray a windowside booth. The patrons scramble for cover. Two waiters root under a counter for shotguns and pistols. One, wearing a ruffled shirt and bow tie, lets the buckshot rip, and the gun's kick knocks him backward. Diners grab their weapons and file outside like a trained SWAT team. A woman straggles behind, swiping a tip from an evacuated table. Seems like they've run through this fire drill plenty of times.

We're watching a drive-by shooting at the Tri Hau restaurant in Garden Grove, California, as recorded by a security camera. A patron, or maybe the owner, has an enemy among Orange County's Vietnamese gangs, and in this neighborhood, this is how you have an argument.

"Shooting? What shooting? We've never had any shootings," insists a Tri Hau waiter during a visit a few weeks later. The restaurant's shattered windows have been replaced and reinforced with thick Plexiglas slabs. A protective shield rims the cash register. The waiter titters, shifting his weight. "We never have any problems."

Roughly 800,000 Vietnamese now live in the U.S., and two of every five live in California. As new immigrants pour in, they're drawn to the more entrenched communities, especially the sun-soaked business centers of Orange County.

Considered the nation's most conservative turf, it is home to Disneyland, Robert Schuller's Crystal Cathedral and the Nixon Library. Evangelists and

ILLUSTRATION BY MEL ODOM

4.

127

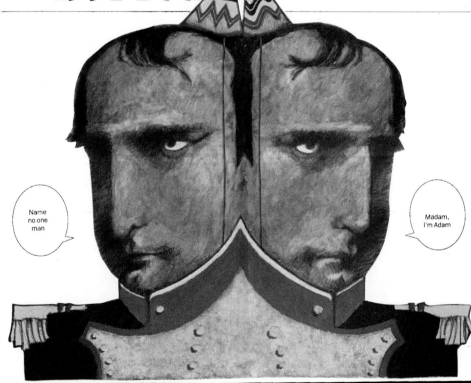

Front page of Lifestyle section.

DESIGN FIRM:

Dayton Daily News, Dayton, Ohio

DESIGNER/ILLUSTRATOR:

Ted Pitts

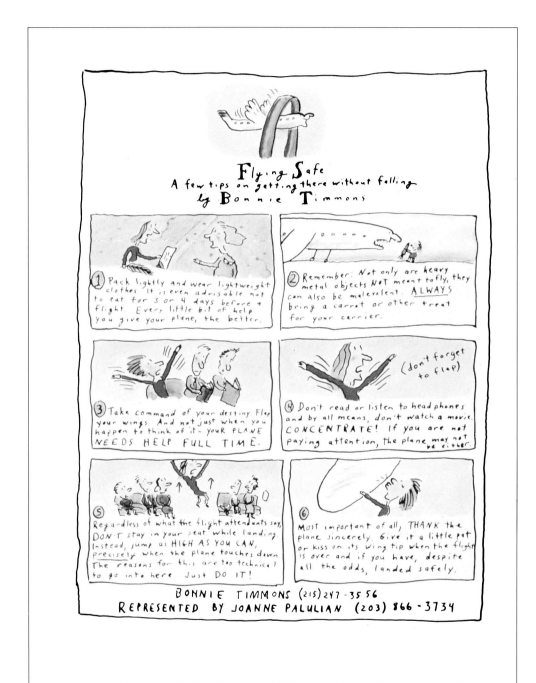

Self-promotion piece.

DESIGNER/ILLUSTRATOR:

Bonnie Timmons,

Coatesville, Pennsylvania

Get celery without stalking the city.

Fresh produce, now at **7-ELEVEN**

Ad.

AGENCY:

J. Walter Thompson/Chicago,

Chicago, Illinois

GROUP CREATIVE

DIRECTORS: Ernie Cox,

Tenney Fairchild

ART DIRECTOR:

Bob Kovanda

PHOTOGRAPHER:

Dave Jordano

COPYWRITER: Larry Lipson

Ad campaign.

AGENCY:

Arian, Lowe, Travis &

Gusick Advertising, Inc.,

Chicago, Illinois

ART DIRECTORS/

COPYWRITERS:

Mike Fornwald, Gary Gusick

ILLUSTRATOR:

Nicole Hollander

Everfresh Juice Company

CD covers.

DESIGN FIRM:

Rounder Records,

Cambridge, Massachusetts

DESIGNER: Nancy Given

ILLUSTRATORS: John Scott

(1), Bill Isles (2)

1.

Rounder Records

DAVID DOUCET "Quand J'ai Parti"

2.

Cover of annual directory of
restaurant, hotel, airport
and limousine services.
AGENCY: The Baker Agency,
Dallas, Texas
ART DIRECTOR/
DESIGNER/ILLUSTRATOR:
Jim Foster

Editorial page.

DESIGN FIRM:

C.W. Publishing, Inc.,

Framingham,

Massachusetts

ART DIRECTOR/

DESIGNER: Nancy Kowal

ILLUSTRATOR:

Normand Cousineau

EDITOR-IN-CHIEF:

Bill Laberis

EDITOR: Joanne Kelleher

Self-promotion piece.

ILLUSTRATOR:

Mark Rosenthal, Malden

Bridge, New York

INTO THE STORM

AT MAMMOTH, HALF-DESERTED FORT
HOOD, THE LAST OF THE TROOPS RUSH
TO JOIN IN A FARAWAY DESERT WAR.

EVEN IN WARTIME, NO GUARDHOUSE OR SECURITY GATE BLOCKS the way into Fort Hood. Traffic rolls onto the giant post unimpeded and unexamined. But the street sign at the first intersection is enough to tell a visitor that this is a different world from the freeway he has just left. It reads, "Tank Destroyer Blvd."

Tanks and destruction are what Fort Hood is all about. Army literature still refers to Fort Hood in anachronistic cold war terms—the largest armored post in the free world. Bounded by Killeen on the east and Copperas Cove on the west, extending northward almost to Gatesville, Fort Hood occupies 339 square miles, making it bigger than eight Texas counties. Its 785 miles of roads, laid east to west, would span Texas. On the post are seventeen lakes, five elementary schools, and the largest commissary in the world, with 25 checkout lanes. Most of the property, however, is hidden from view north of a ridgeline slashed by tank trails that lead into a training wilderness. In normal times the air would be throbbing with the buzz of Apache helicopters and the rumble of M1 tanks and Bradley armored personnel carriers, and motorists would be paying close heed to the yellow diamond-shaped road signs that warn of tank crossings, but these are not normal times at Fort Hood. An Army base is at its most peaceful when the Army is at war.

Before Operation Desert Storm, 37,000 soldiers worked here. Now the main part of the base is an unpeopled as a college campus that has been abandoned by all but a few graduate stu-

dents between semesters. Indeed, many parts of Fort Hood look more like a college than a traditional Army base. The old wooden barracks have been demolished and replaced by brick dormitories and apartments with semiprivate rooms and gaily painted blue railings on outside staircases. But their occupants are gone. On North Avenue, where motor pools for tanks, personnel carriers, and other vehicles of war stretch for three miles, most of the yards contain just a few trucks. The only activity is in the "birdbath," where National Guard troops training at Fort Hood wash dozens of personnel carriers with high-pressure water cannons. To the east, where Apache helicopters once blanketed a mile-long airstrip, only thirteen remain, looking sleek and benign in their silences. Even the trees near the tank trails look different—a grateful green, instead of chalky white from churned-up dust.

The most obvious signs of war are, in fact, the signs. "Pray for Our Soldiers" urges the marquee of the Fort Hood National Bank, as a postscript to the time and temperature. "We're Proud of Our Armed Forces" reads a red, white, and blue billboard sponsored by defense contractor LTV. A portable sign near the airfield carries information of a family-support briefing; another announces the time and place of "A Tribute to Our Soldiers." Yellow ribbons adorn the message boards of the thirteen pots chapels and abound in the subdivisions on the fringes of the base, where families hope for a quick end to the war in communities with names like Patton Park, Pershing Park, and Wainwright Heights.

Outside the base, at a Shamrock gas station, the wife of a Desert Storm soldier keeps a vinyl mat on the counter so customers can write messages for her to send to her husband's unit. "I've got to fill it up and get it mailed soon," she says, "because I know the war just can't go on much longer." PAUL BURKA.

PHOTOGRAPHS BY MATT MAHURIN

TRAINING TAKES ON A SPECIAL URGENCY WHEN THE THREAT OF CHEMICAL WARFARE LOOMS. WITH THE 1ST CAVALRY DIVISION ALREADY IN SAUDI ARABIA, FORT HOOD IS NOW USED MAINLY BY GUARDSMEN GIRDING FOR BATTLE.

FORT HOOD IS THE LARGEST ARMORED POST IN THE FREE WORLD. THE MASSIVE M1 TANK (RIGHT) WILL SPEARHEAD A GROUND ASSAULT, WHILE HELICOPTERS LIKE THE COBRA (ABOVE) AND THE APACHE TRY TO DESTROY ENEMY TANKS.

Editorial spreads.

DESIGN FIRM:

Texas Monthly, Austin,

Texas

ART DIRECTOR/

DESIGNER: D.J. Stout

PHOTOGRAPHER:

Matt Mahurin

FOR A MODERN WARRIOR ON AN OVERNIGHT PATROL, EVEN A PRIMITIVE TOOL CAN COME IN HANDY. THERE WILL BE LITTLE USE FOR AN AX IN THE DESERT, BUT TENTS WILL BE ESSENTIAL EQUIPMENT WHEN THE DAYS GET WARMER.

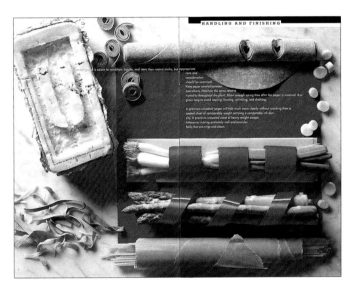

Spreads from "Recipes"

paper promotion.

DESIGN FIRM:

Katz Wheeler Design,

Philadelphia, Pennsylvania

ART DIRECTOR: Joel Katz

PHOTOGRAPHER:

Seymour Mednick

PRINTER: Stinehour Press

Direct-mail self-promotion.

ILLUSTRATOR:

Ward Schumaker,

San Francisco, California

DESIGN FIRM: Design Metro

DESIGNER: Sara Rogers

WRITER: Chuck Carlson

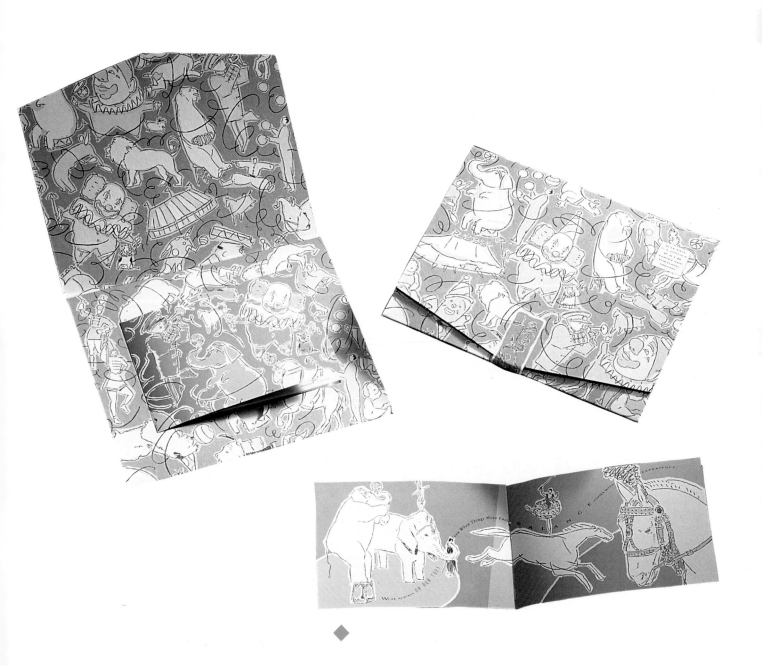

Client brochure sent out by

Equity Research

Department.

DESIGN FIRM:

Donaldson, Lufkin &

Jenrette, New York,

New York

ART DIRECTOR: Paul Waner

DESIGNER: Donald Giordano

ILLUSTRATOR:

Richard Waldrep

Rono Graphic Communications (Printer)

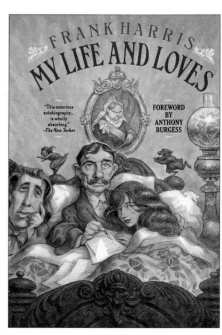

Book cover.

ART DIRECTOR:

Kristina Skalski

ILLUSTRATOR:

Peter de Sève, Brooklyn,

New York

How and why John Deere is working
behind the scenes to help make rural America
a great place to live and work

Strengthening the Rural Fabric

Cathy Leeper flips the switch of her computer in the Hawkeye Technical College lab in Waterloo, Iowa, and opens her John Deere textbook. At Hawkeye, Leeper is preparing herself for a career in agriculture.

Unfortunately for agribusinesses like John Deere, she is in the minority. The agricultural downturn of the 1980s discouraged many students from seeking ag careers. Now, at a time when John Deere dealerships are facing a shortage of trained personnel, colleges, high schools and extension programs are methodically eliminating agriculture courses. The United States Department of Agriculture projects a 3,000 annual shortage of college graduates for some 46,000 jobs in agriculture through 1995.

John Deere has been working on a broad basis for many years to strengthen the image of agriculture and help young people and adults prepare for productive roles in our food, fiber, energy, and natural resource work force. Here are some of the ways John Deere supports rural educational and leadership organizations.

Educational Support Material: Twenty-five years ago, Tom Rader, now a John Deere retiree, spearheaded a program at Deere & Company that affected the education and training of generations of Americans. Rader supervised the writing and publishing of the first comprehensive textbooks on fundamental technology offered to schools and colleges.

"We saw a demand for basic training material at our dealerships," he says. "In the process of putting them together, we found a need for this information in schools around the country. It's still an achievement I'm proud of. I was creating something to meet a company need that also helped the public. What more could an employee ask for?" Teaching support material like the *Fundamentals of Service* and *Fundamentals of Machine Operation* textbook series developed by pioneers like Rader continues to be used at every level of education.

"John Deere provides an excellent base in the areas of business management, equipment maintenance and repair, machinery operation, and record keeping," says Dave Blencha, an instructor at Hawkeye Tech. "Our technical programs have used John Deere educational materials for years."

College Programs: The Postsecondary Agricultural Students Organization (PAS) probably wouldn't exist without John Deere's support," says Ken Olcott, PAS director. The PAS is open to students in two-year technical programs, and is a potential major source of human resources for John Deere dealerships and other businesses.

John Deere also sponsors the PAS Ag Machinery Service Technician Award. Teams of college students test their abilities to adjust, diagnose problems and fix machinery during the awards program at the annual PAS National Conference.

"John Deere was the first company to support our programs," says Olcott. "We try to help the student prepare for the real world. John Deere has provided financial support, but more important, has given us personnel contributions. It means a lot to a student to work directly with someone from John Deere."

Future Farmers of America (FFA) and 4-H: Rick Malir, a John Deere consumer products territory manager, spends most of his time at independent Consumer Products dealers in Iowa and Illinois. Six years ago, Malir held the office of National FFA president.

"When I was in office," says Malir, "it was a down time for agriculture. But when you see a big company like John Deere at the National FFA Convention career show, it makes you realize there are jobs out there. John Deere's involvement with groups like the FFA definitely has a positive impact on people in many ways."

"John Deere has been a sponsor of the

19

Deere & Company (Farm Equipment)

Cover and editorial spread

from company magazine.

ART DIRECTOR/

DESIGNER: Tom Sizemore

ILLUSTRATOR:

Doug Knutson

EDITOR: John Gerstner

Call-for-entries poster for

design competition.

AGENCY:

Keiler Design Group,

Farmington, Connecticut

CREATIVE DIRECTOR:

Mike Scricco

DESIGNER:

Elizabeth Dziersk

ILLUSTRATOR:

Brad Holland

STRATHMORE RENEWAL

RAINFOREST

DESIGN COMPETITION

1.

2.

First (1) and second (2)

printings of promotional

poster for touring

production.

ART DIRECTOR/

DESIGNER/ILLUSTRATOR:

Scott McKowen, Lansing,

Michigan

Spreads from a series of
excerpts from books about
their authors' experiences
in foreign countries.

DESIGN FIRM:

San Francisco Focus

Magazine, San Francisco,

California

ART DIRECTOR/

DESIGNER: Mark Ulriksen

ILLUSTRATORS: Sue Coe (1)

Stefano Vitale (2)

SOUTH AFRICA

A SEARCH FOR LIFE AMONG THE RUINS

BY ADAM HOCHSCHILD

1.

HAITI

A FORTY-YEAR JOURNEY THROUGH HEAVEN AND HELL ON EARTH

PORT-AU-PRINCE ERASED THE DISTINCTION between heaven and hell. It served nicely as both, and included chaotic misery along with the grace, that predatory graciousness, of the wealth found as you moved up the hillsides into purer air, the Canape Vert and Pacot districts, and then farther up toward Petionville, the suburb of the rich.

In town, the gingerbread houses of the old elite seemed to be spun out of spaghetti and lace and sugar candy, mincing and flirting and shivering in the jaws of the termites, an architectural erasure of sense. It was appropriate to a world where people flew like birds, sent messages without wire or words, sang, "Caroline A-cao, dance till it hurts, O! Just dance until it hurts, O!"

Streams of the poor wandered through elegant Petionville, like ants in a fine house. Harborside in Port-au-Prince, in the Martissant District, the rich established little outposts of luxury, elaborate fortress and fantasy mansions, complete with walls protected by broken glass and barbed wire. Protective servants lounged at the gates day and night.

Outside their gardens, often only a few steps away, there were terrains vagues of rotting mangoes, dead chickens, tangled underbrush, and charcoal cooking fires for the lean-to shacks of those lucky enough to find work as helpers to the blessed. The rich swarm through this sea

almost as if the poor were invisible. It was said that many elite Haitians could make love without embarrassment in a space where servants provided drinks or food or simply waited to be summoned. A friend asked, "Would you be troubled, mon cher, to embrace your wife in the presence of a dog or chicken?"

ONE OF THE GREAT PRIMITIVE PAINTERS OF HAITI, A MAN of enormous originality and pride, decorated his house with his own drawings, with paintings and sculpture by his friends, with relics of Catholic and voodoo art, with flowers and plants from his neighborhood—and, in the place of honor on the wall, a full-page photograph of Harold Stassen, clipped from an ancient copy of Life. In a voodoo temple, near a Menorah with candles burning, I

For Herbert Gold, what began as part of a scholarly endeavor in 1953 has become an obsession. In four decades Gold has been to Haiti "perhaps twenty-five times," was once asked to be its consul in San Francisco, and was banned from entering the country for seven years because of reports he wrote about conditions during the regime of François "Papa Doc" Duvalier. "Haiti is poorer than ever now," he says, "but the spirit of the people endures." These excerpts, selected from his forthcoming book, Best Nightmare on Earth, begin with some of Gold's impressions from 1954.—The Editors

BY HERBERT GOLD

2.

Editorial spread from
publication sponsored by
American Diabetes
Association.

DESIGN FIRM:

Tom Suzuki, Inc., Falls
Church, Virginia

ART DIRECTOR: Tom Suzuki

DESIGNER: Timothy Cook

ILLUSTRATOR:

Vivienne Flesher

American Diabetes Association

Impotence is a
condition fraught
with fear, but facing
it may lead you to
treatment that can
change your life.

TREATING
Impotence

Impotence is one of those subjects that evokes fear and misunderstanding. Concern about impotence, of course, is reasonable. But fear and ignorance are often the greatest enemies faced by those who deal with impotence. The fact is, if you have a fear about impotence, facing it is probably one of the best things you can do to change and improve your life.

But first it will help to have a clear understanding of impotence. Impotence is the consistent inability to achieve or sustain an erection of the penis that is sufficiently rigid to penetrate the vagina and continue on to sexual intercourse. Impotence is not an occasional failure of erection, but sustained failure. It is not a premature ejaculation, a decrease in libido or sexual desire, or a failure of ejaculation or orgasm, although all of these can be associated with impotence.

An estimated 10 million men in the general population have experienced impotence, and some experts believe that's just the tip of the iceberg. Men who have diabetes, however, have a special reason to learn about impotence, because it oc-

by Stanley N. Cohen

Diabetes Forecast December 1991

Spreads from *Violent Cases*,
a graphic novel.

DESIGN FIRM:

Tundra Publishing, Ltd.,

Northampton,

Massachusetts

DESIGNER/ILLUSTRATOR:

Dave McKean

AUTHOR: Neil Gaiman

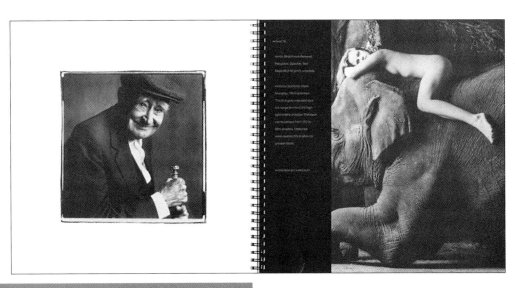

Strathmore Paper Company

Cover and spread from

paper promotion.

AGENCY:

Keiler Design Group,

Farmington, Connecticut

DESIGNERS: Mike Scricco,

Elizabeth Dziersk

PHOTOGRAPHERS:

Lee Crum (1), John

Casado (2)

COPYWRITERS: Mel Maffei,

David Haskell

ABOUT FACE ON STRATHMORE

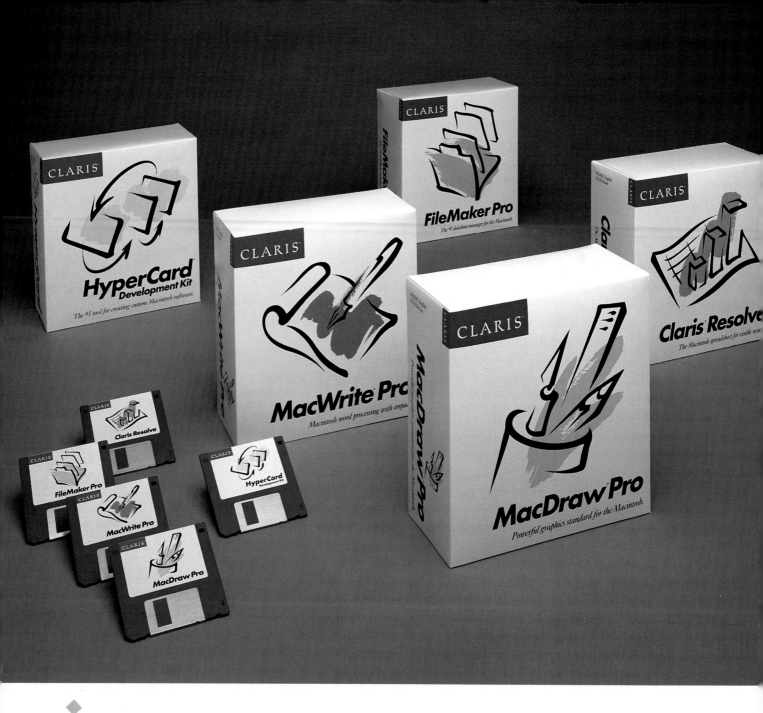

Claris Corporation (Computer Software)

Software packaging.

DESIGN FIRM:

Neumeier Design Team,

Atherton, California

ART DIRECTOR/

DESIGNER: Marty Neumeier

DESIGNERS: Chris Chu,

Curtis Wong

ILLUSTRATOR: Curtis Wong

Poster for a benefit

performance of *Hot L*

Baltimore.

DESIGN FIRM:

Weber Design Partners,

Denver, Colorado

DESIGNER: Christina Weber

PHOTOGRAPHER:

Gary Isaacs

Series of book covers.

ILLUSTRATOR:

Cathleen Toelke,

Rhinebeck, New York

ART DIRECTOR:

Joseph Montebello

DESIGNER: Suzanne Noli

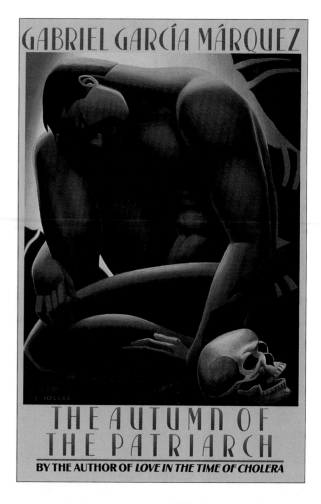

Harper Collins Publishers

Spreads (2,3) from
capabilities brochure for a
mental health center for
children. Self-promotion
poster for the illustrator (1)
using another illustration
from the brochure.

DESIGN FIRM:

Dearwater Design,

Houston, Texas

ART DIRECTOR/
ILLUSTRATOR:

Andy Dearwater

PRODUCTION COMPANIES:

The Beasley Printing

Company (2,3), Stefik

Company (1)

WRITER: Susan Smith

1.

2.

3.

Cover and spreads from direct-mail piece aimed at convention planners.

AGENCY:

Borders, Perrin & Norrander, Portland, Oregon

ART DIRECTOR: Kent Suter

PHOTOGRAPHER:

Michael Jones

COPYWRITER: Greg Eiden

This is a Portland, Oregon, hotel *before* July.

This is a Portland, Oregon, hotel *after* July 1.

Book Portland's *soft second half*, and we'll turn sardines into *salmon*.

Spread from promotional

brochure.

ILLUSTRATOR: John Craig,

Soldiers Grove, Wisconsin

DESIGN FIRM:

Gordon Mortensen Design

ART DIRECTOR/

DESIGNER:

Gordon Mortensen

Stanford University

ch agent is a program, as in OOP, its behavior is now constrained by and to fulfill the promises it has to other agents, carry out its long-commitments, and respond appropriately to incoming messages. There is the assumption of mutual cooperation among friendly agents. If, for example, agent A receives a request that agent B to perform a certain action, and if A has the capability to perform the action and believes B to be really, then A commits to doing what is asked.

Ultimately, Shoham envisions communities of agents interacting smoothly and functioning cooperatively in a wide range of applications, including robotics, air traffic control, and global information searches among networked data bases. He cites the example of a car stopping at an intersection. "There's an explicit communication happening here," he says. "The car is telling the stoplight that it's reached the intersection, and that it intends to stop by triggering the appropriate sensors. There are certain social roles being obeyed here: The car must obey the stoplight. It's making a request to turn, at some point, the stoplight will grant the request. Why not have a link

between the devices that allows the car to communicate with the stoplight from three blocks away, or that allows cars to communicate between one another?"

Reaching the long-range objectives of the AOP project requires not only the development of computationally effective programming languages with appropriate representations of mental state, but also the incorporation of social structure and social rules.

"Think of a society of robots that are supposed to plan paths in a moderately crowded environment," Shoham says. "If each robot plans and executes his path independently of the others, you inevitably get collisions. So we need in place social laws in the domain, like traffic laws, that on the one hand guarantee a minimum of conflict—ideally, ruling out collisions altogether—but on the other hand still allow the robots to achieve their goals in an efficient way. In our daily life, 'Drive on the right' and other traffic rules present a reasonable compromise between these considerations. We need to strike a similar balance for artificial agents."

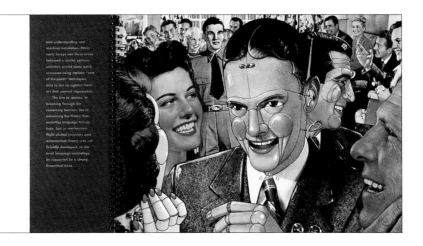

Greeting card.

DESIGNER/ILLUSTRATOR:

Leanne Mebust,

Albuquerque, New Mexico

ART DIRECTORS:

Diana Larson Stuart, Robin

Younger

Missing You

Flavors and Memories of America's Hometowns

SLOW FOOD

MICHAEL JAMES

Book cover.

DESIGN FIRM:

Warner Books, New York,

New York

ART DIRECTOR/

DESIGNER:

Jackie Merri Meyer

ILLUSTRATOR:

Douglas Smith

Cover and fold-out of

product promotion flyer.

ILLUSTRATOR:

Jacqui Morgan, New York,

New York

DESIGN FIRM: Grey-Direct

ART DIRECTOR/

DESIGNER: Fran Coletto

IBM

Cover and fold-out of poster mailer.

DESIGN FIRM:

Jacques Auger Design Associates, Coral Gables, Florida

ART DIRECTOR:

Jacques Auger

DESIGNER: Peg Faimon

ILLUSTRATOR:

Jaime Correa (computer artist)

University of Miami Architecture School

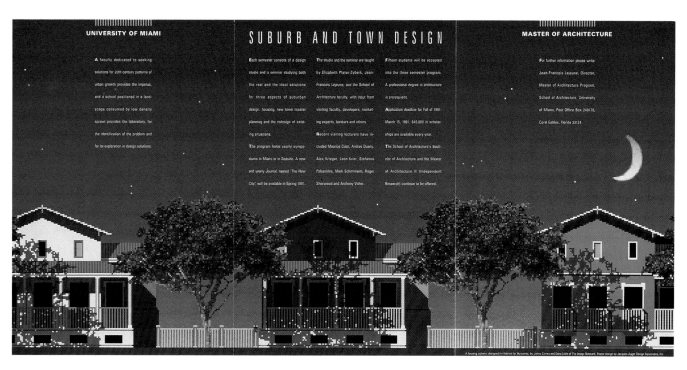

Photograph and spreads
from capabilities brochure.

DESIGN FIRM:
EDS Corporate
Communications, Plano,
Texas

CREATIVE DIRECTOR:
Dick Mitchell

ART DIRECTOR/
DESIGNER: Gary Daniels

PHOTOGRAPHER:
Jay Dickman

ACCOUNT EXECUTIVE:
Gwen Johansen

PRINT PURCHASER:
Lisa Schwab

EDS (Information Technology)

Spread from book *Powerful
Days*.
DESIGN FIRM:
Stewart, Tabori & Chang,
Inc., New York, New York
ART DIRECTOR/
DESIGNER: Jim Wageman
PHOTOGRAPHER: Charles
Moore

Hard-core marchers
huddle by an early
morning fire. Some
three hundred went
the entire distance,
camping by the road.
Other marchers re-
turned to their homes
at night or slept in
motels.

184

185

159

Editorial spread.

DESIGN FIRM:

The Weller Institute for the

Cure of Design, Inc., Park

City, Utah

ART DIRECTOR/

DESIGNER/ILLUSTRATOR:

Don Weller

OF MAMMOTH BONES AND HUMPLESS CAMELS

THE ICE AGE IN PARK CITY

BY DR. WADE E. MILLER

Park City, 40,000 B.C.

A chorus of croaking frogs diminishes as the summer sun first lights the Wasatch Mountains. Runoff from these peaks and hills has provided an abundance of water to a basin that flourishes with wildlife.

Startled by the too-close approach of a swimming muskrat, a pair of mallard ducks takes hurried flight from the waters of the marsh where they spent the night. A minor chain reaction ensues. Anticipating danger, a covey of sage hens feeding on a nearby bank bursts into the air. Three water shrews quickly swim for cover. Having just come up from his hole to inspect the new day, a gopher quickly retreats. A nearly grown litter of deer mice scurry for protection, while both a cottontail and jackrabbit accelerate in opposite directions. But this time it's just a false alarm. The real danger is lurking in tall reeds not far distant. Adjacent to the marsh lies a sagebrush-interrupted grassland that extends to the foot of

ILLUSTRATION BY DON WELLER

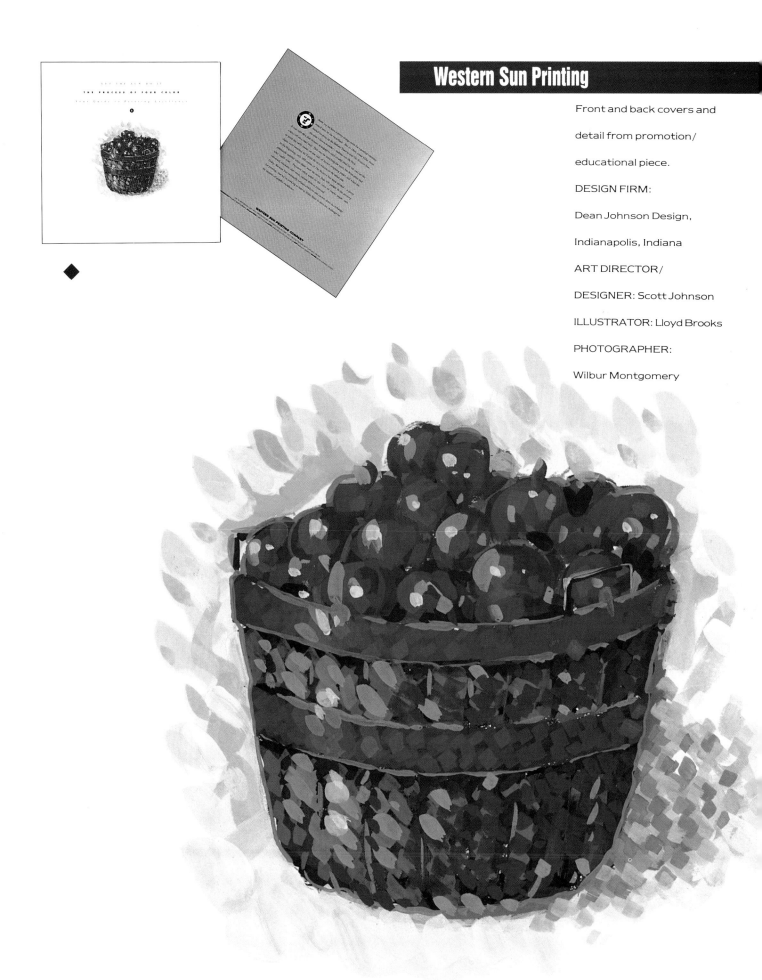

Front and back covers and

detail from promotion/

educational piece.

DESIGN FIRM:

Dean Johnson Design,

Indianapolis, Indiana

ART DIRECTOR/

DESIGNER: Scott Johnson

ILLUSTRATOR: Lloyd Brooks

PHOTOGRAPHER:

Wilbur Montgomery

Promotional poster for

soybean-based inks.

DESIGN FIRM:

Intralink Film Graphic

Design, Los Angeles,

California

CREATIVE DIRECTOR:

Anthony Goldschmidt

ART DIRECTOR/

DESIGNER: Jerry Goen

PHOTOGRAPHER:

Peter Darley Miller

162

Movie poster.

DESIGN FIRM:

Universal Pictures,

Universal City, California

CREATIVE DIRECTOR:

David Sameth

ART DIRECTOR:

Tom Martin

DESIGNER: Barbara Kolo

PHOTOGRAPHER:

Todd Gray

LOGO DESIGN: Art Sims/

11:24 Design

Universal Pictures

Illustration for an article in the company magazine describing a world cruise with an emphasis on the social, political, cultural and physical effects of geography.

ILLUSTRATOR: Ed Lindlof,
Austin, Texas

DESIGN FIRM:
Pentagram Design, Inc.

ART DIRECTOR: Kit Hinrichs

DESIGNER: Allyson Merkley

Book cover.

ILLUSTRATOR: Ed Lindlof,

Austin, Texas

DESIGN FIRM: Dutton

ART DIRECTOR/

DESIGNER: Neil Stuart

Spread announcing CEO of
the year issue and banquet.
ILLUSTRATOR:
Barton Stabler, Florham
Park, New Jersey
DESIGN FIRM:
McFadden Holdings
ART DIRECTOR/
DESIGNER: Alma Phipps

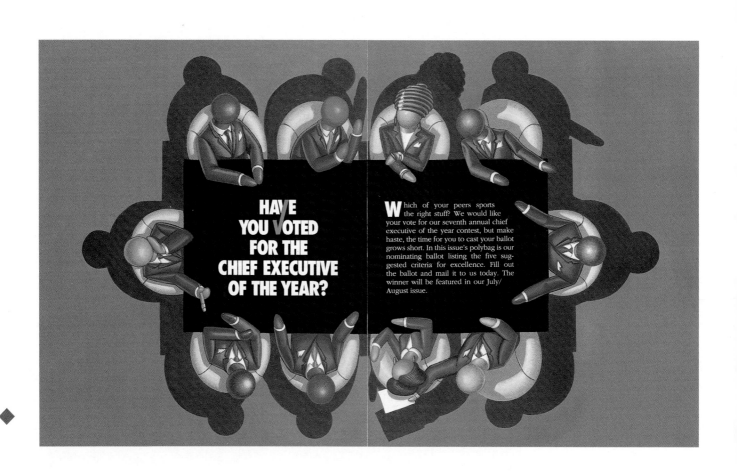

HAVE
YOU VOTED
FOR THE
CHIEF EXECUTIVE
OF THE YEAR?

Which of your peers sports the right stuff? We would like your vote for our seventh annual chief executive of the year contest, but make haste, the time for you to cast your ballot grows short. In this issue's polybag is our nominating ballot listing the five suggested criteria for excellence. Fill out the ballot and mail it to us today. The winner will be featured in our July/August issue.

Chief Executive Magazine

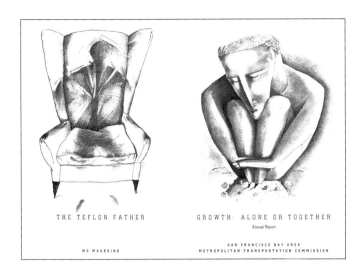

THE TEFLON FATHER

GROWTH: ALONE OR TOGETHER
Annual Report

MS MAGAZINE

SAN FRANCISCO BAY AREA
METROPOLITAN TRANSPORTATION COMMISSION

Self-promotion pieces.

ART DIRECTOR/

DESIGNER/ILLUSTRATOR:

Whitney Sherman,

Baltimore, Maryland

Self-promotion ad later used as direct-mail promotion.

DESIGN FIRM: Schmeltz & Warren, Columbus, Ohio

ART DIRECTOR/ DESIGNER: Crit Warren

PHOTOGRAPHER: George C. Anderson

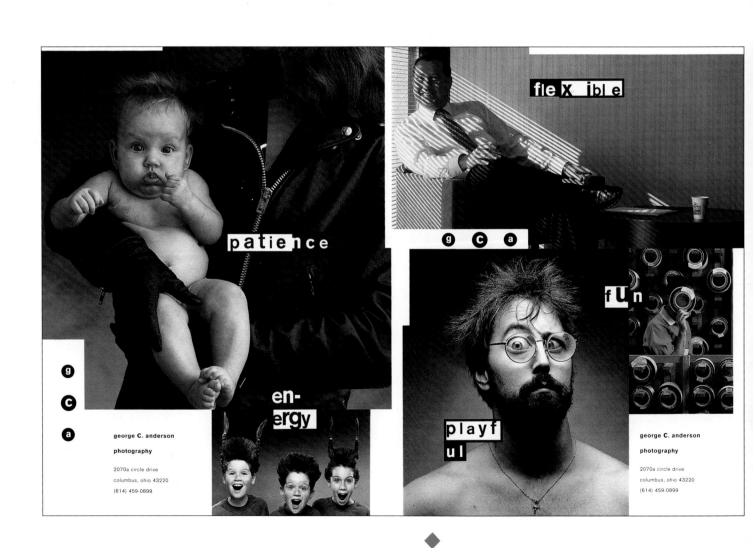

Series of magazine covers.

DESIGN FIRM:

Maria Stroster Graphics,

Chicago, Illinois

ART DIRECTOR:

Cornelia Tuite

DESIGNER/ILLUSTRATOR:

Maria Stroster

Special Real Estate Issue

"If you think that you can think about a thing, inextricably attached to something else, without thinking of the thing it is attached to, then you have a legal mind."
Thomas Reed Powell, American educator, 1880-1955

"For where the rights of men are equal, every man must finally see the necessity of protecting the rights of others as the most effectual security of his own."
— Thomas Paine, 1737-1809

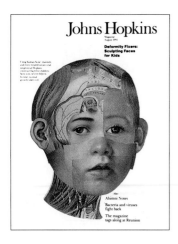

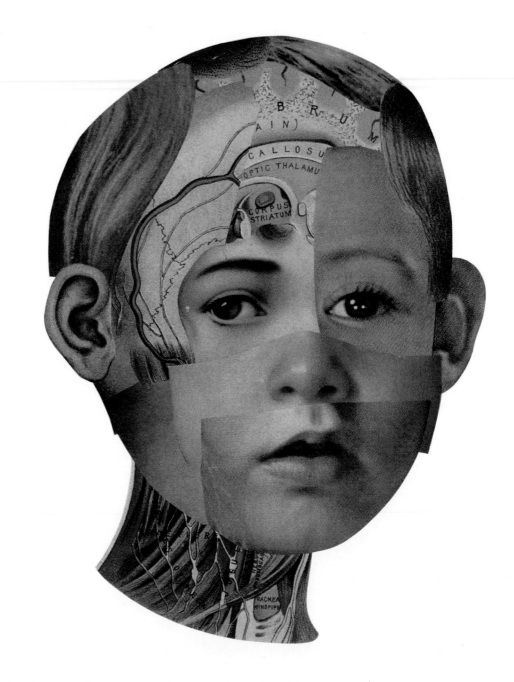

Cover.

ILLUSTRATOR:

Melissa Grimes, Austin,

Texas

ART DIRECTORS:

Royce Faddis, Claude

Skelton

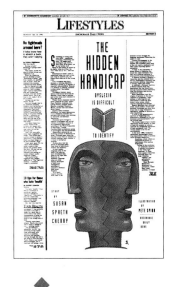

Front page of Lifestyles

section.

DESIGN FIRM:

Anchorage Daily News,

Anchorage, Alaska

DESIGN DIRECTOR:

Galie Jean-Louis

DESIGNER/ILLUSTRATOR:

Pete Spino

JAMES FINNEY BOYLAN

THE PLANETS

A NOVEL

Book cover.

DESIGNER/ILLUSTRATOR:

James Steinberg,

Worcester, Massachusetts

ART DIRECTOR: Frank Metz

Simon & Schuster (Publishing)

Book cover.

ILLUSTRATOR: Jim Sullivan,

Jersey City, New Jersey

ART DIRECTOR/

DESIGNER: Doris Burowsky

St. Martin's Press (Publishing)

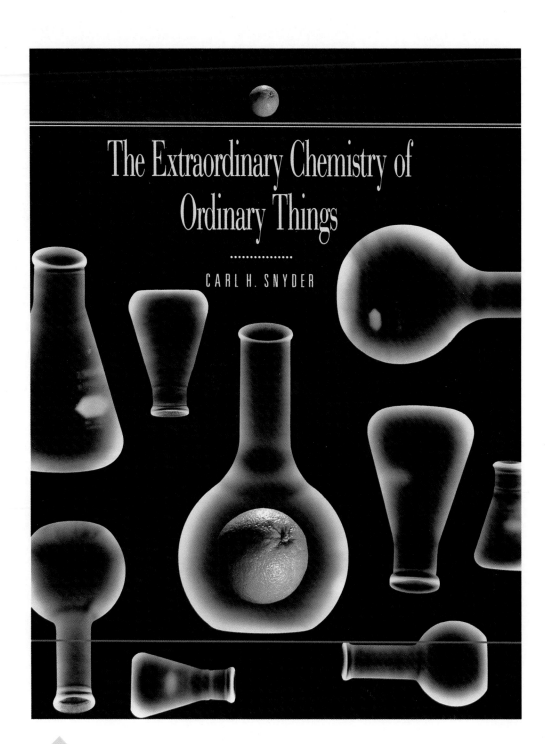

Book cover.

DESIGN FIRM:

John Wiley & Sons, Inc.,

New York, New York

ART DIRECTOR/

DESIGNER:

Karin Gerdes Kincheloe

PHOTOGRAPHER:

Bill Westheimer

"Start off with a head of our fresh-cut lettuce—we have iceberg, romaine, red leaf, green leaf and Boston to choose from—add a few of our juicy tomatoes and slice up a couple of our crisp cucumbers, throw them all together in a large bowl, add some fresh ground pepper, pour some oil & vinegar on—and before you know it, you've got the makings of a classic salad you just may not want to share with anyone."

E. Cecchi Farms
ROUTE 57, FEEDING HILLS

"Everything you'd grow if you had 40 acres."

"Fresh, native asparagus—so sweet and tender that sometimes I don't even bother to cook it—but then, I've never turned down Nani's asparagus quiche, piping hot from her kitchen, either."

E. Cecchi Farms
ROUTE 57, FEEDING HILLS

"Everything you'd grow if you had 40 acres."

"My father and my brothers are always growing new things to try out, but when they told me they were growing black pansies, I thought 'no one is going to buy a black pansy'—until I saw one in bloom. A delicate little blossom that looks like black velvet, with just a touch of violet in the center—we've really grown to love it, and we think you will too."

E. Cecchi Farms
ROUTE 57, FEEDING HILLS

"Everything you'd grow if you had 40 acres."

E. Cecchi Farms

Newspaper ad campaign for family farm.

DESIGN FIRM: DRC Design, Feeding Hills, Massachusetts

ART DIRECTOR/

DESIGNER/COPYWRITER:

David Cecchi

ILLUSTRATOR:

Linda Schiwall

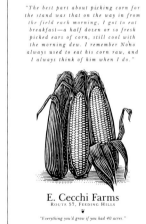

"The best part about picking corn for the stand was that on the way in from the field each morning, I got to eat breakfast—a half dozen or so fresh picked ears of corn, still cool with the morning dew. I remember Nono always used to eat his corn raw, and I always think of him when I do."

E. Cecchi Farms
ROUTE 57, FEEDING HILLS

"Everything you'd grow if you had 40 acres."

"I guess raspberries are an adult food, because when I was a kid, I didn't know of any others my age that liked them—they were fuzzy and had too many seeds. Now, as an 'adult', I could eat them forever, and judging from the way they disappear from the stand as soon as we bring them in from the field, I guess all the kids I grew up with feel the same way."

E. Cecchi Farms
ROUTE 57, FEEDING HILLS

"Everything you'd grow if you had 40 acres."

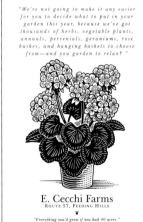

"We're not going to make it any easier for you to decide what to put in your garden this year, because we've got thousands of herbs, vegetable plants, annuals, perrenials, geraniums, rose bushes, and hanging baskets to choose from—and you garden to relax?"

E. Cecchi Farms
ROUTE 57, FEEDING HILLS

"Everything you'd grow if you had 40 acres."

"It seems everyone has their own theory when it comes to telling if a canteloupe is ripe. There are knockers, shakers, thumb-thumpers, and one woman who won't buy a melon unless a dime fits in the stem.(?!) Well, I really don't know about all that—Pop taught me a long time ago that melons turn yellow when they're ripe. The yellower a melon is, the riper it is—hasn't faiten me yet—Pop's a pretty smart guy."

E. Cecchi Farms
ROUTE 57, FEEDING HILLS

"Everything you'd grow if you had 40 acres."

Packaging for series of piano study courses on video.

DESIGN FIRM: Ogdemli/Feldman Design, North Hollywood, California

ART DIRECTOR: Shan Ogdemli

DESIGNERS: Nancy Harasz, Shan Ogdemli

ILLUSTRATOR: Shan Ogdemli

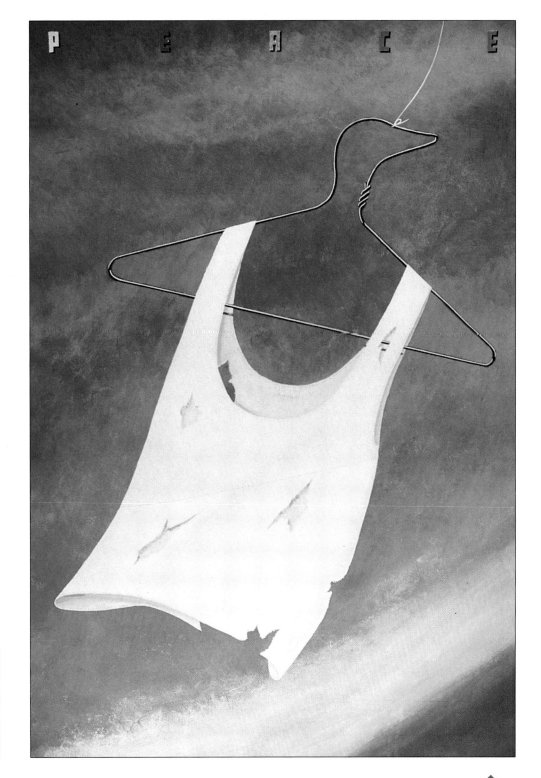

Posters for peace
campaign.

DESIGN FIRM:

Morita Graphic Design, Cos

Cob, Connecticut

ART DIRECTOR/

DESIGNER/ILLUSTRATOR:

Minoru Morita

JAGDA (Japanese Association of Graphic Designers)

Recruitment poster sent to

high schools.

ILLUSTRATOR: Fred Lynch,

Lexington, Massachusetts

DESIGN FIRM:

Gilbert Design Associates

ART DIRECTOR:

Joseph Gilbert

M O V I N G W E S T

Daniels Printing
45 West 45th Street, N.Y., N.Y. 10036, 212·704·2121

Moving announcement

poster.

ILLUSTRATOR: Fred Lynch,

Lexington, Massachusetts

DESIGN FIRM:

Kaminsky Design

ART DIRECTOR:

Tom Kaminsky

Cover.

DESIGN FIRM:

Memphis Magazine,

Memphis, Tennessee

ART DIRECTOR/

DESIGNER: Murry Keith

ILLUSTRATOR: Tim Gabor

Editorial spread.

DESIGN FIRM:

Governing Magazine,

Washington, DC

ART DIRECTOR:

Peggy Robertson

DESIGNER:

Richard Steadham

ILLUSTRATOR:

Theo Rudnak

Promotional postcards for computer program and typefaces.

DESIGN FIRM:

Woods & Woods,

San Francisco, California

CREATIVE DIRECTOR:

Russell Brown

ART DIRECTORS:

Russell Brown, Paul Woods

DESIGNERS: Paul Woods,

Alison Woods

ILLUSTRATOR: Paul Woods

Adobe Software

Cover and spread from

company magazine.

AGENCY:

Gagarin/McGeoch

Advertising, Redwood City,

California

ART DIRECTOR:

Denny Gagarin

DESIGNER: Mark McGeoch

ILLUSTRATOR:

David Tillinghast

Consolidated Freightways (Shipping)

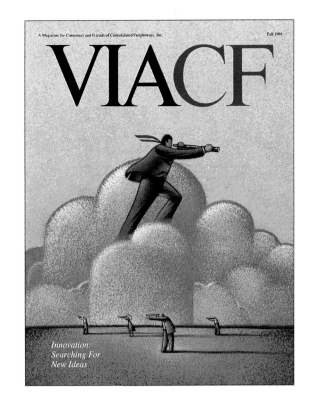

A Magazine for Customers and Friends of Consolidated Freightways, Inc.

Fall 1991

VIACF

*Innovation:
Searching For
New Ideas*

Innovation plays a valuable role in the CF organization, and has been an important part of our success since 1929. Below are some significant milestones in CF's history.

1929
Leland James, the son of a river pilot, founds Consolidated Truck Lines in Portland, Oregon. He acquires several local freight companies operating in the Pacific Northwest.

1932
Six-wheel truck and six-wheel trailer combinations had boosted the possible payload to 39,000 pounds. Additional cube was provided by extending the body of the truck out over the cab.

INNOVATION

Searching
For New
Ideas

Everything that can be invented has been invented," said Charles Duell, director of the U.S. Patent Office in 1899. "Who the hell wants to hear *actors talk?" said Harry M. Warner, of Warner Brothers Pictures, c. 1927.* "Heavier-than-air flying machines are impossible," said Lord *Kelvin, President, Royal Society, c. 1895.* These statements illustrate the inherent resistance people have to change. Change makes people uncomfortable because it means breaking out of an established way of thinking or of doing something and exploring the unfamiliar. Yet, in American industry, innovation is of paramount importance in order to remain competitive.

How can you, a logistics professional, learn to unlock your creativity and that of your staff, so you can excel at your job, and help give your company a competitive edge? First, it helps to understand the origin of your resistance, to look at techniques for stimulating your imagination and to learn to identify where innovation opportunities exist.

In *A Whack On The Side Of The Head*, author Roger von Oech lists ten attitudes that inhibit creativity. By understanding the sources of these attitudes, you can learn to modify them.

There is only one right answer. From the time we are in kindergarten to the time we graduate from high school or college, we are taught that there is only one right answer. "Why bother to think of more than one?" we ask ourselves. "An idea is like a musical note," writes von Oech. "In the same way that a musical note can only be understood in relation to other notes (either as a part of a melody or a chord), an idea is best understood in the context of other ideas. If we have only one idea, we don't have anything to compare it to." In learning to be more creative, it is important to seek many solutions, not just one.

That's not logical. Being creative requires both "soft" and "hard" thinking. "Soft" thinking—based on humor and fantasy—is used in the imaginative phase of the creative process. "Hard" thinking—based on logic and precision—is used in the practical phase. Von Oech writes, "In the imaginative phase we ask questions such as 'Why not?' What

1939
The corporate name of the company is changed to Consolidated Freightways, Inc. This is part of an innovative plan by which a group of motor carriers, known as the Freightways organization, interchange equipment to better service the customer.

1947
CF builds the Freightliner No. 162, one of the first "cab-over-engine" Freightliner trucks. It was built in Portland exclusively by CF for its motor carrier fleet. An innovative design, the "cab-over-engine" was developed by CF's founder, Leland James, for the special demands of moving over the highway freight.

Be a rule breaker: Put practicality aside to discover new and imaginative solutions.

6

7

Modern Dog (Graphic Design)

Self-promotional bus posters.

DESIGN FIRM: Modern Dog,

Seattle, Washington

ART DIRECTORS:

Michael Strassburger,

Robynne Raye, Vittorio

Costarella

DESIGNERS: Robynne Raye

(1), Michael Strassburger

(2), Vittorio Costarella (3)

1.

2.

3.

Ad campaign.

AGENCY: The Puckett Group,

St. Louis, Missouri

ART DIRECTOR:

Terry Finley

PHOTOGRAPHERS:

Chuck Shotwell, Peter

Shepley

COPYWRITER:

Rich Wolchock (1), Steve

Puckett (2)

"Call me callous, call me insensitive, but something about all those fleas and ticks going down the drain really cracks me up."

PURINA
PRIORITY

If you want your customers to smile all through flea and tick season, offer them the guaranteed Priority Tri-Phasial System. Call 1-800-227-8941 for the name of our distributor in your area.

1.

"Either you get some Priority for these fleas of mine or my next nap is in your underwear drawer."

PRIORITY

2.

Cover and spread from

1991 annual report.

AGENCY:

Thomas Ryan Design,

Nashville, Tennessee

ART DIRECTOR/

DESIGNER: Thomas Ryan

ILLUSTRATOR:

Paul Ritscher

PHOTOGRAPHER: McGuire

COPYWRITER: John Baeder

Spread and detail from

paper promotion.

DESIGN FIRM:

Morava Oliver Berté, Santa

Monica, California

ART DIRECTOR: Jim Berté

DESIGNER:

Deanna Kuhlmann

PHOTOGRAPHER:

Everard Williams, Jr.

ILLUSTRATOR:

Joel Nakamura

COPYWRITER:

Donna Freiermuth

Snack and candy packaging

DESIGN FIRM: Michel Design,

South Salem, New York

ART DIRECTOR/

DESIGNER: Deborah Michel

ILLUSTRATOR:

Judith Sutton (1), Charles

Waller (2)

COPYWRITER: Bruce Michel

Shipping box.

DESIGN FIRM:

Metzdorf, Inc., Houston,

Texas

ART DIRECTOR/

DESIGNER/ILLUSTRATOR:

Lyle Metzdorf

Farming Technologies (Food)

CREATIVE DIRECTORS DESIGN DIRECTORS ART DIRECTORS DESIGNERS

CLIENTS